500

jams & preserves

500

jams & preserves

the only compendium of jams & preserves you'll ever need

Clippy McKenna

APPLE

A Quintet Book

First published in the UK in 2013 by
Apple Press
74-77 White Lion Street
London, N1 9PF

www.apple-press.com

ISBN: 978-1-84543-500-4
QTT.FHJP

This book was conceived, designed and produced by
Quintet Publishing Limited
6 Blundell Street
London N7 9BH
United Kingdom

Food Stylist: Maud Eden
Photographer: Jon Whitaker
Art Director: Michael Charles
Series Editor: Donna Gregory
Publisher: Mark Searle

10 9 8 7 6 5 4 3 2 1

Printed in China by 1010 Printing International Ltd.

contents

introduction

Mankind has always preserved food in various forms; from the simplest forms of dried meats to the elaborate sugared fruits of the Renaissance era royals, from beer and wine to jewel-like jars of jams and jellies, preserving is the only way to keep the bounty of a harvest for more than a few days. A bright marmalade enlivens even the darkest winter's breakfast, and a belly-warming sloe gin is always a welcome sight on a cold evening.

In ancient times, fermenting, pickling in vinegar, and air-drying were the most prevalent methods of preserving, though the first known book of recipes included recipes for jams and preserves was written 2000 years ago by a Roman gastronome, Marcus Gavius Apicius. A huge leap forward came with the mass-production of sugar in the late sixteenth century, and the invention of the vacuum seal in the eighteenth century started a new boom in homemade jams, pickles, and liqueurs.

A recent resurgence in artisan jam- and preserve-making has paved the way for companies, such as Clippy's, to make jams and preserves that are based on more fresh fruit and less sugar. See www.clippys.com for more information. And a revival of home-grown produce and preserving is a welcome development!

This book provides all of the recipes you could need to preserve garden or market produce. Enjoy picking out recipes to make, and make sure to read this introductory section before you start; it's packed with tips and guidance to make sure you make the perfect preserve every time.

before you start

Always follow the recipes exactly; they are carefully calibrated to ensure a good set and a long-lasting preserve. Likewise, it's not advised to double up recipes; if you wish to make more, do it in separate batches.

It really is essential to follow very basic, but very strict hygiene rules in order to prevent the spoilage of your preserves.

- Make sure that you have a spotlessly clean kitchen environment; this also extends to your equipment and utensils.
- Always wash hands before and during preparation to minimize bacteria and mould.
- Always wear appropriate clothing; this includes long sleeves and covered shoes (not sandals).
- Always use fresh fruit and vegetables without any blemishes; this extends to spices and herbs as well.
- The filling of jars can be particularly hazardous; please make sure you are aware of your surroundings. Use gloves and a jam funnel. While children can be involved in the preparing of fruit and vegetables, it's best to keep young children at a safe distance while hot pans of boiling sugar are around, and while bottling or potting.
- Some preserves reach very high temperatures; therefore, for your own safety please make sure that you remember the basic rules of the kitchen. The fastest relief comes from cold running water — and lots of it! Always seek medical attention for more serious burns.
- Before you can, make sure you have plenty of sterilized jars ready. Always sterilize more jars than you think you'll need.
- Always use glass jars and bottles with tight-fitting, screw-top lids or caps. Plastic bottles are definitely not suitable for homemade preserves.

preserving techniques

There are many techniques for preserving foods, such as smoking, drying, and curing. In this book the recipes focus on preserving with sugar, vinegar, oil, and alcohol. Each preserving technique can be used separately or together to produce delightful preserved concoctions.

sugar

The most widely used fruit preserving technique is with sugar. Sugar is used in jams, marmalades, jellies, chutneys, relishes, and pickles. When preserving, sugar is an integral part of the process; not only does it preserve the product, it also influences the final flavour of the preserve. The general preserving rule of thumb is to use equal amounts of sugar to fruit, but for certain recipes this is not the case. Most of my sugar-based recipes contain more fruit and less sugar, using fruits high in pectin to set the preserve instead.

refined sugars

I tend to use white refined granulated sugar (which is highly processed, as the natural black treacle is stripped from the sugar cane or beet) for jams, jellies, curds, liqueurs, and cordials mainly due to the large crystals, which dissolve quickly and produce lovely silky preserves. When I first started making sweet preserves, I always used unrefined raw organic cane sugar, but I noticed after a period of time that the fresh fruit flavour was masked by the caramel flavour; it also changed the colour so it wasn't bright and vibrant. I have never used jam sugar (sugar with added pectin); it tends to be quite tricky to use.

unrefined sugars

Brown sugars such as demerara, muscovado, and black treacle are wonderful for imparting a more robust flavour to your preserves, and they work exceptionally well in marmalades, chutneys, relishes and some condiments. Due to the manufacturing process, unrefined sugars retain most, if not all, their black treacle flavour.

vinegar

When preserving with vinegar, it's really important to choose vinegars that have an acidity level of at least 5 per cent; you can find this on the label. This will help you preserve and store your preserve correctly; the undesirables (micro-organisms) tend not to survive in this acidic environment. Within this book you'll notice that I use different types of vinegars; each one imparts different flavours, depending on what you're looking for, whether robustness, sharpness, or sweet and sour.

cider vinegar

Derived from apples, this is one of my favourite vinegars, and I tend to use this the most. It's not as expensive as wine vinegars, and it works really well in savoury jellies, pickles, relishes, and most chutneys.

wine vinegars

Both red and white wine vinegars are very delicate, and are excellent when you want to impart a subtle vinegar flavour. I tend to match the colour of the vinegar with the fruit I'm using, for instance white wine vinegar in my Spiced Pears and red wine vinegar for my Spiced Roasted Plum Chutney recipes.

malt vinegar

Malt vinegar, which is derived from barley, produces a really robust preserve and balances the flavours of most fruit and vegetables really well.

flavoured vinegars

You can also use herb-flavoured vinegars, such as tarragon, thyme, and oregano for preserving. Or make your own fruit vinegars such as raspberry and blackberry; simply cook 250ml (9 fl. oz) mashed berries with 200ml (7 fl. oz) red wine vinegar and add to a jelly bag. Strain, and then add 3 tablespoons of sugar to the juice and cook until dissolved; bring to a boil and simmer for 5–10 minutes. Skim the surface and pour into sterilized jars.

oil

Oil is brilliant as a means to effectively seal out the oxygen, thus preventing spoilage by isolating the food from the air. This preserving technique provides a seal that you can also eat. Always be sure to completely cover preserved foods with your chosen oil; never leave any food protruding because this will spoil. Lightly press the food to get rid of any air bubbles and seal tightly.

I love experimenting with oils; the trick is to use the best oil you can afford. You'll soon discover that the oil becomes highly flavoured from the preserved foods and is delicious. I tend to use virgin olive oil because it is unrefined and has a subtle acidity to it; I never use extra virgin because the oil solidifies once cold. You could use sunflower and canola oils, which are less expensive, but for me they don't have the robustness of virgin olive oil.

alcohol

Homemade alcoholic beverages, as far as I'm concerned, are the pinnacle of one's foray into preserving. My earliest memories of my dad were his fruity alcoholic concoctions; they used to reside behind our sofa, carefully placed under woollen blankets to keep warm while they fermented. It was a real treat to behold! So when I was asked to write this book, I had to include my favourite recipes using alcohol. Pay particular attention when making my Elderflower Champagne because if not treated correctly, the fermenting process will have bottles of champagne popping open, and all your hard work will be lost.

Alcohol prevents the growth of undesirable micro-organisms in preserved fruited drinks and drunken fruits. It is important to make sure you use a grain spirit that is at least 40 per cent alcohol (80 per cent proof). My personal favourite is gin; its complex botanicals work so well with most fruits. Vodka works particularly well in my Blood Orange Liqueur and brandy is a perfect partner with cherries for Cherry Ratafia.

equipment

Preserving needn't cost a great deal; most preserves can be made with regular kitchen equipment. Once you get the hang of it, I would recommend buying a maslin preserving pan and other nifty items such as spice mills and blenders, but for now check out the list below.

- Wide-necked jam funnels
- Fruit and vegetable chopping boards, and very sharp knives
- Citrus squeezer
- Large bowls to hold ingredients and to use for extracting the juice for jellies
- Ladles
- A trusty apple peeler & corer
- Nonstick pans that hold a maximum of 2.5 litres (6 pints) with handles that do not get hot
- Long-handled wooden spoons
- Labels for jars — get creative and make your own labels
- Digital scales, measuring spoons, cups, and jugs
- Jam jars/bottles with screw-top lids and caps
- Heatproof gloves
- Preserving pan or wide-bottomed pan
- Preserving or sugar thermometer
- Slotted spoons
- Nylon sieves — don't use metal as this reacts with the acid from the fruits
- Sealing discs. Some preservers use sealing discs all the time. However I have never used them, as long as you fill to the neck of the bottle/jar and seal straight away you won't need them
- Jelly bags and stand

basic techniques

sterilization

It is really, really important to use completely sterile glass jars or bottles to store homemade preserves. Follow these basic rules for every recipe:

- Always wash jars in hot soapy water and then rinse well. Place them upside down on a baking tray and place in a preheated oven (170°C/325°F) for 15–20 minutes; make sure they don't have any soap bubbles inside. Remove from the oven and set aside while making the preserve. Sterilize the lids in a pan of boiling water for 10 minutes and let dry before use.

- You can use the dishwasher to sterilize your containers, but make sure you remove them as soon as the cycle has finished. They need to be dry without any condensation.

- If using recycled jars/bottles, make sure they are cleaned inside as well as outside and are free from cracks or chips, because this is a potential breeding ground for micro-organisms to grow.

- To remove old labels, fully immerse the jars in hot water for 20 minutes. Then use a blunt knife to scrape off the label. To remove any residual glue, use a cotton ball and nail polish remover.

- Always fill jars right to the top. Preserves cool when they shrink, and this causes a vacuum in which no micro-organisms can grow.

- Make sure there are no visible air bubbles.

- To get a really good seal, wear rubber gloves when tightening lids.

labeling and jars sizes

I love making preserves but always forget to label them, so I often find hidden gems lurking in the backs of cupboards or refrigerators without labels. While this can be great fun, by labeling them with the date/year/name of the preserve, you'll always know exactly what you have.

- You can buy all kinds of self-adhesive labels, or you can visit your local craft shop to pretty up your preserves. We've given you ideas for this throughout the book.

- Always label your preserves when they are cold. When the jars are hot, the glue melts and the labels will not stick.

- Each recipe has an approximate yield at the top of the recipe. This will enable you to work out how many jars to sterilize.

- I find that small to medium jars are the best ones for storing and using. However, I do love using Kilner jars in sizes up to 500g (1lb) for presentation and gift-giving purposes.

- Always sterilize extra jars just in case you need them.

testing for a set

Use any of these tests to check preserves are ready for potting:

- Flake test (above, left): Dip the spoon into the jam. Hold it over the pan and twirl it around three times; let the mixture fall. If it falls like a sheet, it's ready; if it dribbles, it's not.

- Plate test (above, center): Place a small drop on a cold plate and leave for 1 minute. Gently push through the mixture. If it wrinkles and doesn't ooze back, it's ready.

- Blob test (above, right): Dot a blob of jam onto a cold plate. If it holds its shape without spreading, it's ready.

- Thermometer test: Place the thermometer in the preserve after you have reached the rolling boil stage. Make sure you keep it away from the sides and bottom of the pan; otherwise you'll get a false reading. You want to reach a temperature of 102–105°C (215–221°F). Leave it in position until you reach your required temperature. I personally prefer the methods above.

storage & shelf life

Storing preserves correctly will maximise their shelf life. As soon as you have finished potting and sealing your preserves, place them in a cool, dark area and do not touch them for at least a day. Once opened, always replace the seal correctly. Always store opened preserves in the refrigerator and consume within 2–4 weeks, and discard the whole container of any contaminated (i.e. mouldy) preserves.

Unless stated otherwise in specific recipes, follow these storage guidelines for all preserves in this book:

jam and jellies	use within 1 year
fruit curds and oil-based condiments	use within 4 weeks; store in the refrigerator
fruit cheeses and butters	use within 6 months
marmalades	use within 2 years
fruit liqueurs	use within 2 years
bottled fruits	see individual recipes
cordials	use within 2 weeks
relishes, pickles, ketchup, and mincemeat	use within 1 year
chutneys	use within 1–2 years, but let mature for 2–4 weeks
honeyed nuts and mustards	use within 6 months

troubleshooting

I've been making and teaching how to make preserves for a number of years, and I have come across all manner of problems. This has enabled me to put together a list of top spoilers. This list may look overwhelming, but my advice is to choose a recipe and then read through this section, so that you get an idea of how to stop the things that are going wrong.

mould prevention

- Always can your preserves hot or cold; never warm.
- Always sterilize your glass jars/bottles. See pages 12–13 for instructions.
- Never store jars/bottles in a warm environment. Store them in a cool, dark place straight after potting, right until opening.
- Always make sure you follow the recipe exactly.
- Always use clean, ripe fruit; never use blemished or mouldy fruit and vegetables, as this can lead to spoilage in your preserves. If you pick the fruit yourself, make sure that you pick the fruit when it's dry and not on a damp or wet day.
- Keep fingers out of the jar/bottles and lids when potting.
- Fill right to the rim of the jar/bottle and apply the cover right away; this will avoid any airborne bacteria settling on top of your preserve.
- If you do have mould growing, never scoop it off or ignore it; as moulds and fungi grow, they can produce harmful mycotoxins that can be harmful if eaten. Discard any jars that have mould in them.

dull colours in preserves

- Your preserve should look bright and beautiful; if it is dull, then the preserve was overcooked either before the sugar was added or at the final boil.

fruit and herbs floating to the top

- To stop fruit and herbs floating to the top of your preserves when potting, leave the preserve in the preserving pan for about 5–10 minutes, then stir to distribute and can into cooled jars.
- Make sure to add enough sugar; too little will result in too thin a preserve.
- Make sure to can only when the setting point (correct temperature) is reached.

chewy fruit and tough peel in jams and marmalades

- When cooking jams, it is really important to add the sugar at the right time. For instance if you add sugar to gooseberries or blackcurrants before the skins are soft and malleable, the sugar only makes the fruits chewy in the final preserve.
- When cooking marmalades, only add the sugar when the peel is sufficiently soft; take some peel, cool it, and rub it through your fingers. If it breaks up easily, go ahead; if not, continue to simmer.

crunchy jam or sugar crystals in your preserves

- Always make sure you add your sugar at a medium temperature and stir to distribute the sugar. Make sure it is fully dissolved before cranking up the heat for the rolling boil.
- Always follow the recipe within this book. Too much sugar can turn your lovely preserve to a jar of crunchy jam!
- Overcooking can lead to crystals forming in your preserves.

setting problems

- If the preserve is runny, the pectin of the fruit was likely not high enough. Some fruits are low in pectin, and others are high in pectin. For example, strawberry jam needs an extra pectin boost from lemons or from another pectin-rich fruit like gooseberries, redcurrants, or apples.
- Always add the stated amount of sugar. It can be tempting to skimp on sugar in the name of a healthier preserve. Sugar is the main setting agent, along with pectin-rich fruits, to achieve the correct set for jam, jellies, and marmalades.

- If you end up with a preserve that's too runny, it won't store well. It's not generally possible to remedy this, and I would suggest using the preserve as a delicious sauce.

- If you use frozen fruit, always make sure you add extra fruit or sugar as freezing the fruit destroys the natural pectin found in the fruit.

- Make sure to get jam, jelly, or marmalade to a full rolling boil. Make sure the surface is covered in a mass of tiny bubbles that do not recede when you stir them. Time your preserve at this stage for setting. Do not stir because this cools the preserve, and it will take longer to set.

- Never add too much water, especially for juice extraction for jellies; make sure you follow the exact quantities stated in the recipe.

cloudy jellies

- Leave to strain the juice overnight; if you try to speed up the process by squeezing the bag, your jelly will become cloudy.

- Don't wait too long to pour jellies into jars; use a wide-necked jam funnel and pour in as soon as your preserve is ready to pot.

- Using artificial sweeteners or underripe fruit can make jellies cloudy.

bubbles dispersed within the preserve

- If there are bubbles in your preserve, this can be due to scum that has not been removed correctly; use a slotted spoon.

- Make sure you stir the correct way when removing the scum (i.e., the same way around); otherwise, you'll introduce more air into preserve.

shrinking away from sides of jars

- This occurs when the preserve has been over-boiled or an airtight seal has not been created when covering the jars. Make sure the lid is secure and tight.

jams

The most famous and universally beloved of all
preserves, a jam simply consists of lightly cooked
soft fruits and sugar heated together until it
resembles the sweet, sticky, gooey goodies that we
know and love. In this chapter, the recipes range
from the classic strawberry jam to a cheeky
chocolate & banana jam. Enjoy!

old-fashioned strawberry jam

see variations page 36

Strawberry jam can be very difficult to set, and you may need to add extra pectin. Mashing the strawberries helps to release the pectin, ensuring a good set.

500g (1 lb 2 oz) strawberries (hulled)
5 tbsp. lemon juice
400g (14 oz) sugar

Place the strawberries and lemon juice into a pan. Gently simmer and cook until the berry juice begins to run, approximately 5–10 minutes. Then take a potato masher and gently mash the strawberries.

Add the sugar, stirring until it is all dissolved (if you do not dissolve the sugar before the final boil, sugar crystals will form in the jam).

Bring to a rolling boil; the jam should be ready in 3–5 minutes. Remove from the heat and test for a set.

Once the setting point is reached, remove any scum. Cool the jam for 5–10 minutes. This will ensure that if there are any whole pieces of strawberries, they will not float to the top of the jam jar. Pour the warm jam into cooled, sterilized jars and seal tightly.

Makes 800g (1 lb 7 oz)

summer fruit jam

see variations page 37

Peaches and roses herald the arrival of summer, so along with strawberries, raspberries and blackberries, I've added a small amount of rose water to enhance the flavour.

225g (8 oz) peaches
5 tbsp. lemon juice
1 tbsp. water
225g (8 oz) blackberries

225g (8 oz) raspberries
225g (8 oz) strawberries
1 tbsp. rose water
800g (1 lb 10 oz) sugar

Place the peaches in the boiling water; leave for 30 seconds and then remove and carefully place them in cold water. Take the peaches out and remove the skins; cut them in half and discard the stone. Try to keep the peach juice. Chop the peaches and add them to the pan with the lemon juice and water. Gently simmer until soft. Add the remaining fruit and rose water. Gently simmer until the colour runs from the raspberries, blackberries, and strawberries, or until they are soft but have retained their shape. Add the sugar, stirring until it is all dissolved – if you do not dissolve the sugar before the final boil, you will get sugar crystals forming in the jam.

Bring the fruit mixture to a rolling boil (do not stir jam at this stage because this reduces the heat and upsets the setting point); the jam should be ready in 3–5 minutes. Remove from the heat and test for a set. Once the setting point is reached, remove any scum. Cool the jam for 5–10 minutes. This will ensure that if there are any whole pieces of fruit, they will not float to the top of the jam jar. Pour into cooled, sterilized jars and seal.

Makes 1.5kg (3 lbs 5 oz)

cheeky chocolate & banana jam

see variations page 38

This jam is superb with thick buttered toast and croissants. It makes an excellent topping for cupcakes and victoria sponge cake layered with jam and whipped cream.

800g (1 lb 10 oz) ripe bananas (about 6 large)
250ml (9 fl. oz) water
400g (14 oz) vanilla sugar or regular sugar

120g (4 oz) dark chocolate (70 per cent cocoa solids), chopped
2 tbsp. almond liqueur or almond essence

Thinly slice the banana, and place in a large pan with the water and sugar. Mix well on a medium heat until the sugar has melted. Stir constantly and bring the mixture to a full rolling boil. The mixture may well have a slight grey hue; this will disappear.

Keep the mixture at a rolling boil for 2 minutes, stirring constantly until the mixture becomes clearer and brighter. Once the bananas become soft and increase in size, add the dark chocolate. Mix well and gently melt the chocolate. Once melted, bring the mixture back to a boil and then remove from the heat immediately. Stir in the almond liqueur or essence.

Ladle the hot jam into sterilized jars. The jam will keep up to 3 months if stored in the refrigerator. Once opened, consume it within 2–3 weeks — if it lasts that long!

Makes 1.3kg (2 lbs 14 oz)

toffee apple jam

see variations page 39

This is a fantastic way to use up apples and the addition of the homemade toffee sauce enhances the vanilla apple jam. It's a perfect topping for ice cream.

for the toffee sauce
100g (3½ oz) light brown muscovado sugar
4 tbsp. corn syrup
1 stick unsalted butter (room temperature), chopped
4 tbsp. double cream

for the apple jam
1 lb 5 oz cooking apples (peeled & cored weight)
120ml (4 fl. oz) water
1 vanilla pod
2 tbsp. lemon juice
200g (7 oz) sugar

Make the toffee sauce: Melt the sugar, syrup, and butter in a small pan and bring slowly to the boil. Reduce the heat and simmer for 3 minutes, or until thick. Remove from the heat and stir in the cream; set aside to cool.

Make the apple jam: Place the apples, water, vanilla pod seeds, and lemon juice in a separate pan and cook down until soft and fluffy — about 10–15 minutes. Once the apples have become soft, add the sugar over a low heat until all the sugar has dissolved. Then turn up the heat and bring to a simmering boil for approximately 4–5 minutes. The apple jam should be lovely and thick. (Be careful because this jam has a tendency to spit.) Set aside to cool.

Add a layer of toffee sauce to the bottom of the jar and then a layer of apple jam and continue layering until you reach the top of the jar. Consume within two weeks.

Makes 1.1kg (2 lbs 6 oz)

strawberry petal fizz jam

see variations page 40

Summer lasts as long as you want it to with this perfectly preserved jam. Dried rose petals add a really intense rose flavour.

½ package dried rose petals
4 tbsp. lemon juice
2 tbsp. rose water

600g (1 lb 5 oz) strawberries (hulled)
450g (1 lb) sugar
3 tbsp. pink sparkling wine

Macerate your rose petals with a little sugar, half the lemon juice, and the rose water, for at least an hour before you make the jam. Then cook the strawberries and remaining lemon juice until the strawberries are soft.

Once the fruit has become soft but has not lost its shape, add the rose petal mixture to the fruit, then stir in the sugar on a low heat and wait until it has dissolved. Once it has dissolved, turn up the heat and keep on a rolling boil until the setting point is reached, approximately 5 minutes.

Once the setting point is reached, remove any scum. Add the pink sparkling wine and cool the jam for 5 minutes. This will ensure that the fruit does not float to the top of the jam jar when it is poured into the sterilized jars. Jar, and store for a couple of days. Once opened, place in the refrigerator and eat within the month.

Makes 1kg (2 lbs 4 oz)

cherry bomb jam

see variations page 41

The highlight of this jam comes from the addition of grappa, which provides a robust flavour. Cherries have little or no pectin, so I've included redcurrant juice and reduced the sugar.

500g (1 lb 2 oz) ripe dessert cherries
225g (8 oz) redcurrants
150ml (5 fl. oz) water

500g (1 lb 2 oz) sugar
3½ tbsp. grappa or almond essence

Wash and stone the cherries (or you can cook the cherries whole and then scoop out the cherry stones before the rolling boil). Put the redcurrants in a pan with half the water and bring to a simmering boil. Cook for half an hour and then remove and strain the redcurrant liquid through a sieve.

Add the redcurrant juice and the cherries to a medium pan. Gently boil the cherries until they are soft and tender (make sure that the cherry skins are soft before you add the sugar otherwise the skins will become hard when setting), then add the sugar and slowly bring the mixture to a rolling boil. Once the sugar has dissolved, turn up the heat and keep on a rolling boil until the setting point is reached, approximately 5 minutes.

Finish by stirring in the grappa or almond essence, and let rest for 5 minutes to ensure the fruit doesn't rise to the top of the jar. Once rested, add the jam to the sterilized jars and seal. Leave the jars in a cool dark place for a couple of days.

Makes 1.2kg (2 lbs 8 oz)

rosy raspberry jam

see variations page 42

I named this jam after my daughter, Rosie! This is her favourite jam. Raspberries and rose water are a match made in heaven; enjoy the gorgeous smell wafting through your home.

225g (8 oz) cooking apples (peeled, cored &
    chopped)
1 vanilla pod, seeds only
4 tbsp. lemon juice

300g (12 oz) raspberries (hulled)
2 tbsp. rose water
350g (14 oz) sugar

Add the apples and vanilla to a large pan and cook until soft and pulpy, then add the lemon juice, raspberries, and rose water to the apples, and then add the sugar on a low heat. Stir and wait until the sugar has dissolved. Once it has dissolved, turn up the heat and keep on a rolling boil until the setting point is reached, approximately 5 minutes.

Once the setting point is reached, remove any scum. Cool the jam for 5 minutes. This will ensure that the fruit does not float to the top of the jar when it is poured into the sterilized jars. Pot and seal. Store the jars for a couple of days. Once opened, place the jam in the refrigerator and eat within the month.

Makes 1.1kg (2 lbs 6 oz)

tutti frutti jam

see variations page 43

Blackcurrants are the super pectin of the jam world. By combining high pectin fruits with low pectin fruits, you can create luscious jam without lots of sugar.

450g (1 lb) blackcurrants (stripped from stalks)
3–5 tbsp. freshly squeezed orange juice
450g (1 lb) strawberries (hulled and halved if large)

450g (1 lb) raspberries (hulled)
zest of 1 medium orange
1kg (900g (2 lbs) 4 oz) sugar
3 tbsp. freshly squeezed lemon juice

Put the blackcurrants and orange juice into a preserving pan. Bring to the boil and then gently simmer until the skins are soft, approximately 5 minutes. Add the strawberries, raspberries, and orange zest (take care not to squash the raspberries when stirring), and simmer for another 10 minutes.

Add the sugar, stirring until it is all dissolved. Only add the sugar if the strawberries are soft. Add the lemon juice, and bring to a rolling boil. The jam should be ready in 3 minutes. You can also test by doing the cold plate test or flake test.

Once the setting point is reached, remove any scum. Cool the jam for 5–10 minutes. This will ensure that if there are any whole pieces of fruit, they will not float to the top of the jam jar when it is poured into the sterilized jars. Pour the hot jam into cooled, sterilized jars and seal.

Makes 2kg (24lbs 8 oz)

peachy delight jam

see variations page 44

This jam reminds me of the deep South. I spent a year working and living as a nanny in the US, and my host father was from the home of the famous Annual Peach Jam Jubilee in Chilton, Alabama.

500g (1 lb 2 oz) peaches (about 4–5)
450g (1 lb) nectarines (about 4–5)
3 tbsp. freshly squeezed lemon juice

120g (4 oz) mango (peeled and stone removed)
2 tbsp. water
950g (900g (2 lbs) 2 oz) sugar

Place the whole peaches and nectarines in boiling water, leave for 30 seconds and then remove. Carefully place in cold water. Take the fruit out and remove the skins; cut them in half and discard the stone. Chop the peaches and nectarines and add to a large pan along with the lemon juice, mango and water. Gently simmer until soft.

Once the fruit is soft, add the sugar, stirring until it is all dissolved. Bring to a rolling boil; the jam should be ready in approximately 5 minutes. Remove from the heat and test for a set.

Once the setting point is reached, remove any scum. Cool the jam for 5–10 minutes. This will ensure that if there are any whole pieces of fruit, they will not float to the top of the jar. Pour the hot jam into cooled, sterilized jars and seal.

Makes 1.7kg (3lbs 12 oz)

plumberry jam

see variations page 45

This jam makes the most of the autumn bounty, along with an infusion of fresh vanilla.

225g (8 oz) cooking apples (weight once peeled, cored and chopped)
225g (8 oz) plums (weight once stoned & halved)
3 tbsp. water

225g (8 oz) blackberries (weight once hulled)
1 vanilla pod, seeds only
2 tbsp. fresh squeezed lemon juice
600g (1 lb 6 oz) sugar

Put the chopped apples, plum halves and water into a large preserving pan with the lid on. Bring to a gentle boil and simmer until the plums and apples have broken down (i.e., soft and pulpy), approximately 10–15 minutes. Then add the blackberries, vanilla and lemon juice and cook until the blackberries soften, approximately 5–10 minutes.

Once the plum skins are soft and the blackberries are squishy, add the sugar, stirring until it is all dissolved. Do not replace the lid because you want to reduce the mixture to a jam consistency.

Bring the sugar mixture to a rolling boil; the jam should be ready in 4–6 minutes. Once the setting point is reached, remove any scum. Cool the jam for 5–10 minutes. This will ensure that the whole pieces will not float to the top of the jam jar. Pour the hot jam into cooled, sterilized jars and seal.

Makes 1.1kg (2 lbs 6 oz)

variations

old-fashioned strawberry jam

see base recipe page 19

strawberry & vanilla jam
Add the seeds from one vanilla pod to the strawberries.

strawberry & mint jam
Add 3 sprigs of fresh mint to the rolling boil and discard the mint before potting.

strawberry & black pepper
Sounds odd, but the infusion of strawberry and pepper is a match made in heaven. Add 1 teaspoon of freshly ground black pepper just before potting; stir and pot.

strawberry & orange jam
Add the zest (no pith) and juice from 1 large orange; add at the same time as the strawberries.

queen strawberry jam
If you can get hold of edible gold leaf, add this sparingly just before potting.

variations

summer fruit jam

see base recipe page 21

summer fruit cup jam
Replace the peaches with nectarines (follow the same preparation as for the peaches), and replace the blackberries with another cup of raspberries.

fruity goddess jam
Use the same amount of fruit and replace with blackcurrants, cherries (seeded), oranges (peeled and cut into small pieces) and strawberries (hulled); omit the rose water and replace with orange vodka.

summer berry cobbler
Replace the blackberries with blueberries and add 1 bay leaf (discard when you pot the jam); when cooking the fruit, omit the rose water and replace with seeds from 1 vanilla pod and ¼ teaspoon nutmeg.

apricot jam
Replace the peaches with fresh apricots and then follow the recipe.

variations

cheeky chocolate & banana jam

see base recipe page 22

banoffee pie jam
Add 2 tablespoons of homemade toffee sauce, or toffee pieces, to the jam just before you pot and seal. Omit the alcohol.

banana brown betty jam
Replace the granulated sugar with half dark brown muscovado sugar and half light brown muscovado sugar. Omit the alcohol.

banana caramel jam
Add the juice of 1 lime; replace the granulated sugar with light brown muscovado sugar and a dab of butter. Replace the almond liqueur with rum.

banana & fig jam
Add the flesh from 3 fresh figs to the jam and omit 1 of the bananas.

toffee apple & banana jam
Replace half the bananas with apples and proceed as main recipe.

toffee apple jam

see base recipe page 25

spiced toffee apple jam
Add 1 teaspoon cinnamon, 1 teaspoon apple pie spice, and 1 teaspoon ground ginger to the apple jam and proceed as main recipe.

spiced pear & toffee jam
Replace the apples with pears and add an extra 2 tablespoons lemon juice.

spiced caramel pear jam
Follow the spiced toffee apple jam recipe, but don't allow it to cool as much as the toffee apple recipe. Instead, mix them together and can while hot.

vanilla pear jam
Omit the toffee sauce. Make the pear jam as per the apple jam and use the seeds from two vanilla pods; add 1 tablespoon vanilla vodka at the end of cooking.

variations

strawberry petal fizz jam

see base recipe page 26

appleberry petal fizz
To make this jam go further, add 450g (1 lb) cooking apples (weight when peeled and cored). Chop the apples finely and cook first, before adding the strawberries. Increase the amount of sugar by 200g (7 oz).

very berry citrus jam
Add 2 chopped tablespoons candied orange peel at the beginning of cooking. Omit the rose petals and rose water and replace with 2 tablespoons orange liqueur; add at the end of cooking.

raspberry petal fizz
Replace the strawberries with raspberries.

cherry bomb jam

see base recipe page 29

chili cherry bomb jam
Add 1 teaspoon of dried chili flakes to the redcurrant mixture and strain through a sieve. This will add a touch of heat to the jam; remove the grappa and almond essence from the end.

maraschino cherry jam
Add the seeds from 1 vanilla pod at the beginning of cooking. Replace the grappa with maraschino liqueur.

blueberry cherry jam
Replace 225g (8 oz) of cherries with the same weight of blueberries.

cherry lime jam
Omit the grappa and add the juice and zest from 1 lime at the end of cooking.

cherry & pistachio jam
At the end of cooking add 3 tablespoons of shelled, chopped, unsalted, toasted pistachios; stir to combine and pot.

variations

rosie raspberry jam

see base recipe page 30

honeyed rosie raspberry jam
Replace the sugar with fruit sugar and reduce by one third. Add
3 tablespoons of your favourite honey at the end of cooking before
potting and sealing.

peachberry jam
Replace half the raspberries with the same weight of peaches (skin and chop
into small pieces); omit the rose water and replace with peach liqueur.

nectarine, mango & raspberry jam
Replace half the raspberries with the same weight of nectarines (skin and
chop into small pieces). Add a couple tablespoons of chopped mango at the
beginning of cooking.

jalapeño and raspberry jam
Omit the rose water and replace the apples with the same amount of
raspberries. Add 1 tablespoon chopped fresh jalapeño along with the
raspberries.

variations

tutti frutti jam

see base recipe page 31

fruity elderflower jam
Remove the orange zest and orange juice; add 3 tablespoons elderflower cordial before potting and sealing the jam.

blues bay jam
Omit the strawberries and replace with blueberries; omit the raspberries and replace with cooking apples (peeled, cored and chopped). Omit the orange zest/juice. Add the apples with the blackcurrants; add the blueberries and 2 fresh bay leaves when the blackcurrants and apples are soft. Before potting, remove the bay leaves.

tutti frutti jam
Replace the raspberries with chopped bananas; replace the strawberries with blueberries. Add the bananas and blueberries once the blackcurrant skins are soft.

peachy delight jam

see base recipe page 32

spiced peach delight jam
Add ½ to 1 teaspoon ground cinnamon at the end of cooking and set aside for 2 minutes. Then pot and seal.

peach cobbler jam
Replace the mango and nectarines with peaches; add ½ teaspoon ground cinnamon,¼ teaspoon nutmeg, and seeds from 1 vanilla pod. Add at the beginning of cooking.

bourbon peach jam
Replace the nectarine and mango with peaches; add the seeds from 1 vanilla pod and 1 cinnamon stick at the beginning of cooking. Add 2 tablespoons bourbon just before potting.

peach melba jam
Omit the mango and nectarine and replace with fresh raspberries. Cook the peaches first; add the raspberries just before the sugar, along with the seeds from 1 vanilla pod.

peach & lavender jam
Add 1 teaspoon fresh lavender flowers once the jam is ready to pot.

plumberry jam

see base recipe page 35

ginger plumberry jam
Add 2 or 3 teaspoons diced preserved or crystallized ginger. Omit the vanilla
seed pod from the recipe.

chai–plumberry jam
Take 1 cinnamon stick, 6 cardamom pods, and 8 cloves and place them in a
muslin bag; tie tightly. Add the spice bag to the fruit from the beginning.
Remove the spice bag just when you have reached the setting point.

victoria plum & star anise jam
Replace all the fruit with Victoria plums; remember to add the sugar when
the plum skins are soft. Add 2 star anise when simmering the plums.

plumberry port jam
Add 3 tablespoons port wine at the end of cooking.

marsala plumberry jam
Add 1 cinnamon stick when cooking the apples; remove just before potting.
Add 3 tablespoons of Marsala wine at the end of cooking.

jellies

These clear, bright, jewel-like preserves are a joy to
make and a joy to eat. The whole fruit is cooked
with water to form a pulp which is then extracted
through a jelly bag to produce the fruit juice. This is
heated along with sugar, spices, and/or herbs until
set. Use to enliven sandwiches, complement cheeses
and cooked or cured meats, or enjoy simply on hot,
buttered toast.

apple jelly

see variations page 64

Once you've mastered this apple jelly, move onto the others in this chapter. All the jellies in this chapter follow the same rule; to each 600ml (1 pint) of extracted juice, use 400g (14 oz) of sugar. Remove the scum from the cooked jelly and always pour your jellies carefully into jars using a sterilized jug.

900g (2 lbs) cooking apples (chopped)
600ml (20 fl. oz) water
400g (14 oz) sugar

Place the chopped apples and water in a large saucepan, making sure that they are clean and free from bruises. It is important to simmer gently until the apples are soft and pulpy. From time to time you can stir the fruit and help it along by gently crushing the fruit. Spoon the pulp into a jelly bag that has been attached to the legs of a jelly bag holder. Place a bowl underneath the jelly bag. Then leave it to strain overnight. Leave the fruit pulp in the jelly bag until it is completely dry. (Do not try to squeeze the pulp through the bag; otherwise you will get a cloudy jelly instead of clear and sparkling jelly.)

The next day add 400g (14 oz) of sugar to each 600ml (1 pint) of juice in a pan. Once dissolved, bring to a steady boil and then gently boil for approximately 5–10 minutes, until you have reached setting point. Once the setting point has been reached, pour the apple jelly into cool, sterilized jars before sealing. Use within 12 months. Once opened, refrigerate and use within 4–6 weeks.

Makes 1.5kg (3 lbs 5 oz)

apple & star anise jelly

see variations page 65

The next stage in making apple jellies is to try adding herbs and spices. Star anise has a lovely warm and fragrant aroma.

900g (2 lbs) cooking apples (chopped)
600ml (20 fl. oz) water

400g (14 oz) sugar
2 star anise

Place the chopped apples and water in a large saucepan, making sure that the apples are clean and free from bruises. It is important to simmer gently, until the apples are soft and pulpy. From time to time, you can stir the fruit and help it along by gently crushing the fruit.

Spoon the pulp into a jelly bag that has been attached to the legs of a jelly bag holder. Place a bowl underneath the jelly bag. Then let it strain overnight. Leave the fruit pulp in the jelly bag until it is completely dry. (Do not try to squeeze the pulp through the bag; otherwise, you will get a cloudy jelly instead of clear and sparkling jelly.)

The next morning add 400g (14 oz) of sugar to each 600ml (1 pint) of juice to a pan along with the star anise. Once the sugar is dissolved, bring to a steady boil and then gently boil for approximately 5–10 minutes, until you have reached setting point. Once the setting point has been reached, discard the star anise and pour the apple jelly into cool, sterilized jars and top with the other star anise before sealing. Use within 12 months. Once opened, refrigerate and use within 6 weeks.

Makes 1.5kg (3 lbs 5 oz)

mint jelly

see variations page 66

Apple and fresh mint jelly is a match made in heaven. It's delicious served with grilled Greek halloumi cheese and a green leaf salad.

900g (2 lbs) cooking apples (chopped)
600ml (20 fl. oz) water
400g (14 oz) sugar
1 tbsp. freshly squeezed lemon juice

4 tbsp. white wine vinegar or apple cider vinegar
4 tbsp. chopped fresh mint leaves

Place the chopped apples and water in a large saucepan, making sure that they are clean and free from bruises. It is important to simmer gently, until the apples are soft and pulpy. From time to time, you can stir the fruit and help it along by gently crushing the fruit.

Spoon the pulp into a jelly bag that has been attached to the legs of a jelly bag holder. Place a bowl underneath the jelly bag. Let it strain overnight. Leave the fruit pulp in the jelly bag until it is completely dry. (Do not try to squeeze the pulp through the bag. If you do, you will get a cloudy jelly instead of clear and sparkling jelly.)

The next morning add 400g (14 oz) of sugar to each 600ml (1 pint) of juice in a large pan, along with the lemon juice. Stir. Once dissolved, bring to a steady boil and then gently boil for 2 minutes. Add the vinegar and continue to cook for approximately 5–10 minutes, until it reaches setting point. Add the chopped mint leaves and stir to distribute. Pour the apple jelly into cool, sterilized jars before sealing. Use within 12 months. Once opened, refrigerate and use within 6 weeks.

Makes 1.5kg (3 lbs 5 oz)

redcurrant & chili jelly

see variations page 67

I adore redcurrants; they make a superb jelly. Try adding the jelly to homemade meatballs — truly delicious!

900g (2 lbs) (4 cups) redcurrants (chopped)
300ml (10 fl. oz)
400g (14 oz) sugar

2 medium-sized chilies (chopped)
3 tbsp. red wine vinegar

Place the washed redcurrants and water in a large saucepan. It is important to simmer gently until the berries are really soft and have released all their juice.

Spoon the redcurrant pulp into a jelly bag that has been attached to the legs of a jelly bag holder. Place a bowl underneath the jelly bag. Let it strain for several hours or overnight. Leave the pulp in the jelly bag until it is completely dry. Do not try to squeeze the pulp through the bag. If you do, you will get a cloudy jelly instead of clear and sparkling jelly.

Add 400g (14 oz) of sugar to each 600ml (1 pint) of juice in a pan, along with the chilies. Once the sugar has dissolved, bring it to a steady boil and gently boil for 2–3 minutes. Add the vinegar and continue to boil for approximately 5–8 minutes, until you have reached the setting point. Once the setting point has been reached, let the jelly cool for 5 minutes to distribute the chilies. Then stir and pour the redcurrant jelly into cool, sterilized jars before sealing. Use within 12 months. Once opened, refrigerate and use within 6 weeks.

Makes 1.1kg (2 lbs 6 oz)

raspberry & basil infused jelly

see variations page 68

This is the first jelly I made for some best friends and they loved it. Brilliant with coarse patés, white fish dishes, or eaten on its own with a spoon!

1kg (2 lbs 4 oz) raspberries
175ml (6 fl. oz) water
400g (14 oz) sugar

1 tbsp. freshly squeezed lemon juice
1 large handful basil (including stalks)

Place the raspberries and water in a large saucepan. It is important to simmer gently until the raspberries have released their juices and are soft. From time to time you can gently press the raspberries.

Spoon the pulp into a jelly bag that has been attached to the legs of a jelly bag holder. Place a bowl underneath the jelly bag. Let it strain overnight. Leave the fruit pulp in the jelly bag until it is completely dry. (Do not try to squeeze the pulp through the bag, otherwise you will get a cloudy jelly instead of clear and sparkling jelly.)

Add 400g (14 oz) of sugar to each 600ml (1 pint) of juice in a pan, along with the lemon juice. Once the sugar has dissolved, bring to a steady boil and then gently boil for 2–3 minutes. Add the basil and continue to boil for approximately 5–8 minutes, until you have reached the setting point. Once the setting point has been reached, remove and discard the basil. Stir and pour into cool, sterilized jars before sealing. Use within 12 months. Once opened, refrigerate and use within 6 weeks.

Makes 1kg (2 lbs 4 oz)

blackcurrant & peppercorn jelly

see variations page 69

This jelly is the perfect accompaniment to soft and blue cheeses and cured meats.

1kg (2 lbs 4 oz) blackcurrants
700ml (1¼ pints) water

400g (14 oz) sugar
20 peppercorns

Place the blackcurrants and water in a large saucepan. It is important to simmer gently until the blackcurrant skins are soft to the touch and have released their juices.

Spoon the pulp into a jelly bag that has been attached to the legs of a jelly bag holder. Place a bowl underneath the jelly bag. Let it strain overnight. Leave the fruit pulp in the jelly bag until it is completely dry. (Do not try to squeeze the pulp through the bag, otherwise you will get a cloudy jelly instead of clear and sparkling.)

Add 400g (14 oz) of sugar to each 600ml (1 pint) of juice in a pan, along with the peppercorns. Once the sugar has dissolved, bring to a steady boil and gently boil for 8–10 minutes, or until you have reached the setting point.

Once the setting point has been reached, stir and pour the jelly and peppercorns into sterilized jars before sealing. Use within 12 months. Once opened, refrigerate and use within 6 weeks.

Makes 1kg (2 lbs 4 oz)

blackberry & cinnamon jelly

see variations page 70

The addition of cinnamon to this fabulous deep purple jelly is sweet and aromatic. Perfect for a breakfast treat spread on thick buttered toast.

1kg (2 lbs 4 oz) blackberries
175ml (6 fl. oz) water
400g (14 oz) sugar

2 cinnamon sticks
1 tbsp. lemon juice

Place the blackberries and water in a large saucepan. It is important to simmer gently until the blackberries are soft to the touch and have released their juices.

Spoon the pulp into a jelly bag that has been attached to the legs of a jelly bag holder. Place a bowl underneath the jelly bag. Let it strain overnight. Leave the fruit pulp in the jelly bag until it is completely dry. Do not try to squeeze the pulp through the bag. If you do, you will get a cloudy jelly instead of clear and sparkling jelly.

Add 400g (14 oz) of sugar to each 600ml (1 pint) of juice in a pan, along with the cinnamon sticks and the lemon juice. Once the sugar has dissolved, bring it to a steady boil and gently boil for 8–10 minutes, or until you have reached the setting point.

Once the setting point has been reached, remove and discard the cinnamon sticks. Stir and pour the jelly into cool, sterilized jars before sealing. Use within 12 months. Once opened, refrigerate and use within 6 weeks.

Makes 1kg (2 lbs 4 oz)

cranberry & port wine jelly

see variations page 71

This is a festive treat that is perfect with roasted meats, soft and blue cheeses. It makes a great present for someone who loves food; the colour and smell are amazing.

450g (1 lb) cooking apples
1 lb 5 oz cranberries
400ml (13½ fl. oz) water

400g (14 oz) sugar
6 tbsp. port wine

Place the apples, cranberries and water in a large saucepan. It is important to simmer gently and keep the lid on, because cranberries can jump out of the pan while they are popping. Begin the second stage once the skins of the cranberries are soft to the touch and have stopped popping and the apples are soft and pulpy.

Spoon the pulp into a jelly bag that has been attached to the legs of a jelly bag holder. Place a bowl underneath the jelly bag. Let it strain overnight. Leave the fruit pulp in the jelly bag until it is completely dry. Do not try to squeeze the pulp through the bag. If you do, you will get a cloudy jelly instead of clear and sparkling jelly.

Add 400g (14 oz) of sugar to each 600ml (1 pint) of juice in a pan. Once the sugar has dissolved, bring it to a steady boil and gently boil for 8–10 minutes, or until you have reached the setting point. Once the setting point has been reached, stir in the port wine and pour the jelly into cool, sterilized jars before sealing. Use within 12 months. Once opened, refrigerate and use within 6 weeks.

Makes 1.1kg (2 lbs 6 oz)

orange, lemon & lime jelly

see variations page 72

This is what you call a flavour sensation! It packs a punch and perks up any sandwich with the addition of this mouth-watering, citrus-packed jelly.

900g (2 lbs) cooking apples (chopped)
peel and juice of 3 large oranges
300ml (10 fl. oz) fresh orange juice
peel and juice of 2 lemons

peel and juice of 1 large lime
300ml (10 fl. oz) water
400g (14 oz) sugar

Place the chopped apples, orange, lemon, and lime rind (no pith) as well as the fruit juices and water in a large saucepan making sure that the apples are clean and free from bruises. It is important to simmer gently until the apples are soft and pulpy. From time to time stir the fruit and gently crush it. Make sure the citrus fruit rind is soft to the touch.

Spoon the pulp into a jelly bag that has been attached to the legs of a jelly bag holder. Place a bowl underneath the jelly bag. Let it strain overnight. Leave the fruit pulp in the jelly bag until it is completely dry.

Add 400g (14 oz) of sugar to each 600ml (1 pint) of juice in a pan. Once the sugar has dissolved, bring to a rolling boil and gently boil for 8–10 minutes, or until you have reached the setting point. Once the setting point has been reached, stir and pour the jelly into cool, sterilized jars before sealing. Use within 12 months. Once opened, refrigerate and use within 6 weeks.

Makes 1kg (3 lbs)

spiced three-fruit jelly

see variations page 73

This heady three-fruit combination is packed with tart cranberries, juicy oranges, and soft apples, with a kick of freshly grated ginger.

450g (1 lb) cooking apples
600g (1 lb 5 oz) cranberries
3 large oranges (peel and flesh; no pith or seeds)
300ml (10 fl. oz) fresh orange juice

400ml (13½ fl. oz) water
400g (14 oz) sugar
5cm (2 in.) fresh ginger (grated)

Place the apples, cranberries, orange peel, orange juice, and water in a large saucepan. It is important to simmer gently and keep the lid on, because cranberries can jump out of the pan while they are popping. Begin the second stage once the skins of the cranberries are soft to touch and have ceased popping, and the apples are soft and pulpy.

Spoon the pulp into a jelly bag that has been attached to the legs of a jelly bag holder. Place a bowl underneath the jelly bag. Let it strain overnight. Leave the fruit pulp in the jelly bag until it is completely dry. Do not try to squeeze the pulp through the bag. If you do, you will get a cloudy jelly instead of clear and sparkling jelly.

Add 400g (14 oz) of sugar to each 600ml (1 pint) of juice in a pan. Grate the fresh ginger into the jelly juice and sugar. Once the sugar has dissolved, bring to a steady boil and gently boil for 8–10 minutes, or until setting point has been reached. Pour the jelly into cool, sterilized jars before sealing. Use within 12 months. Once opened, refrigerate and use within 6 weeks.

Makes 1kg (3 lbs)

variations

apple jelly

see base recipe page 47

apple & elderflower jelly
Add 3 small heads of elderflowers to the apples at the beginning of cooking.
Add a couple tablespoons of elderflower cordial before potting.

chili apple jelly
Add 1 teaspoon crushed dried chili flakes with seeds to every 600ml
(20 fl. oz) of extracted apple juice.

old-fashioned apple jelly
Add the zest and juice from 1 large lemon at the beginning when cooking
the apples.

mulled apple jelly
Add 3 tablespoons cider vinegar to the extracted juice. Place 1 cinnamon
stick, 10 allspice berries, and 10 cloves into a muslin bag; tie and place into
the extracted apple juice along with the sugar and boil. Remove the spice
bag once the setting point is reached.

cinnamon apple jelly
Add 3 cinnamon sticks with the cooking apples at the beginning and cook;
strain as per recipe.

apple & star anise jelly

see base recipe page 49

apple & rose petal jelly
Omit the star anise and macerate ½ package of dried rose petals with
1 tablespoon lemon juice and 1 tablespoon sugar overnight while straining
the apple juice. Add to the apple juice extraction with the sugar and proceed
as main recipe.

apple, rosehip & star anise jelly
Add 450g (1 lb) rosehips along with the apples and proceed as main recipe.
This produces a lovely pink hue.

honeyed apple & star anise jelly
Add 5 tablespoons runny honey at the beginning when cooking the apples.

apple geranium jelly
Make sure you use pesticide-free leaves. Add 2 tablespoons washed, chopped
geranium leaves with the apples at the beginning. Omit the star anise.

apple cardamom jelly
Gently bruise 15 cardamom pods to release the oils and add to a muslin bag.
Place into the extracted apple juice along with the sugar; proceed as main
recipe. Omit the star anise.

variations

mint jelly

see base recipe page 50

apple & rosemary jelly
Omit the mint, and add 3 tablespoons chopped fresh rosemary with
3 tablespoons cider vinegar at the end of cooking.

apple & sage jelly
Omit the mint, and add 4 sprigs fresh sage at the rolling boil stage; remove
when potting.

apple & tarragon jelly
Omit the mint, and add 4 tablespoons fresh tarragon leaves to the rolling
boil; remove when ready to pot.

apple & lemon balm
Omit the mint, and add 3 sprigs lemon balm at the rolling boil stage;
omit the vinegar and replace with freshly squeezed lemon juice for some
extra zing.

redcurrant & chili jelly

see base recipe page 53

redcurrant & rosemary jelly
Replace the chilies with 3 chopped sprigs of rosemary; add to the final
2–3 minutes of the last boil.

cumberland jelly
Remove the chilies. When cooking the redcurrants, add 1 large orange and
1 large lemon. Squeeze the juices and slice the citrus fruit; add with the
chopped apples. Once you have extracted the juice, follow the recipe, adding
1 teaspoon each ground ginger and mustard powder to the juice and sugar.
Add 2 tablespoons port before potting.

redcurrant & apple jelly
Replace half of the redcurrants with cooking apples. Proceed as main recipe.

all the reds
Replace half the redcurrants with blood oranges; squeeze out the juice and
slice the oranges. Add with the remaining redcurrants.

super trouper hot jelly
To double the strength of the redcurrant jelly, remove the fresh chilies and
use 2 tablespoons crushed dried chilies.

variations

raspberry & basil infused jelly

see base recipe page 54

raspberry & lemon zest jelly
Replace the basil with the zest of two lemons; add the zest to the last boil
with the juice from the two lemons, including the tablespoon of lemon juice.

raspberry jalapeño
Add 2 tablespoons freshly chopped jalapeños to the extracted raspberry juice
and cook as per the recipe; leave the chilies in at the end.

raspberry rosemary jelly
Add 2 tablespoons chopped rosemary to the extracted juice and cook as per
recipe; do not remove the rosemary. Set aside to cool before potting to
ensure that the rosemary is distributed evenly when you can

blackcurrant & peppercorn jelly

see base recipe page 55

blackcurrant & port jelly
Add 3 tablespoons sherry or port just before you pot the jelly. It gives a new dimension to this jelly.

blackcurrants & cassis
Perfect with soft cheeses. Add 3 tablespoons cassis just before potting.

blackcurrant & apple jelly
To make your blackcurrants go further, replace half the blackcurrants with cooking apples. Cook as per the recipe; omit the peppercorns.

blackcurrant & lemon verbena jelly
This is a match made in heaven. Add the lemon verbena to the extracted juice and sugar; remove when potting. Omit the peppercorns.

miss lavender blue jelly
Add 1 tablespoon dried lavender to the juice and sugar. Omit the peppercorns.

variations

blackberry & cinnamon jelly

see base recipe page 56

spiced blackberry jelly
Add some cloves and allspice berries with the cinnamon stick; tie up in a muslin bag and cook with the blackberries.

all the blues jelly
Add 450g (1 lb) blueberries with the blackberries; proceed as main recipe.

blackberry punch jelly
Add 450g (1 lb) cooking apples with the blackberries. Omit the cinnamon and add a spilt vanilla pod when cooking the extracted juices. Remove the vanilla pod when ready to pot.

barmy blackberry & balsamic jelly
Omit the cinnamon stick and add 4 tablespoons balsamic vinegar just before potting.

cranberry & port wine jelly

see base recipe page 59

cranorange jelly
Add the peel from one large orange to the sugar and extracted juice in the
final boil; discard the peel when the setting point is reached. Replace the
port with 3 tablespoons orange liqueur before potting.

cranberry pear fruit jelly
Add 450g (1 lb) pears with the cranberries. Add a cinnamon stick when
cooking the extracted juices.

zingy cranberry jelly
Add 2 tablespoons freshly grated ginger in the final stage of cooking; omit
the port.

spiced cranberry jelly
Add 1 cinnamon stick, 2 bay leaves, 10 whole cloves, 3 tablespoons cider
vinegar, and the peel from 1 large orange to the extracted juice and sugar.
Omit the port. Before potting, remove the spices and peel.

variations

orange, lemon & lime jelly

see base recipe page 60

orange, lemon, lime & sage jelly
Add some sprigs of sage in the final boil. Once infused and the setting point has been reached, discard the sage and pot the jelly.

citrus & wine jelly
Cook as per the recipe and add 6 tablespoons chablis (or other full-flavoured dry white wine) just before potting.

orange & hibiscus jelly
Omit the lime and lemons; replace with oranges. Add a handful of (rinsed and dried) hibiscus flowers when cooking the juice and sugar. Remove the flowers before potting.

spiced orange, lemon & lime jelly
Add 3 tablespoons dried crushed chili flakes with the juice and sugar.

variations

spiced three-fruit jelly

see base recipe page 63

habañero-spiced three-fruit jelly
Add 2 tablespoons white wine vinegar, half a red onion finely diced, and 3 tablespoons habañero peppers with seeds; cook with the jelly juice extraction until you've reached the setting point. Set aside for a few minutes and pour gently into the jars; seal.

quince jelly
Omit cranberries and replace with quince. Proceed as main recipe.

vanilla three-fruit jelly
Omit the grated ginger and replace with the seeds from 1 vanilla pod; add with the extracted juice and sugar.

spiced three-fruit jelly
Fill a muslin bag with 1 cinnamon stick, 10 cloves, and 8 allspice berries. Add to the extracted juice and sugar. Remove before potting.

fruit curds, cheeses & butters

Relatively low in sugar, but bursting with flavour, fruit curds, butters, and cheeses are a brilliant combination of butter, eggs, and tangy fruits; the cooking temperature is very low so they are usually cooked over a bain-marie. Personally, I adore these little gems, because they're fruity, zesty, and creamy.

blackcurrant & sloe gin curd

see variations page 92

Fruit curds are very delicate little things; don't boil them or the curd will split.

225g (8 oz) cooking apples (peeled, cored, and
    chopped)
3 tbsp. water
1 tbsp. lemon juice
225g (8 oz) blackcurrants

400g (14 oz) sugar
125g (4½ oz) unsalted butter
4 large eggs, beaten well
1 tbsp. sloe gin or cassis liqueur

Place the chopped apples with the water and lemon juice into a pan and cook until soft, fluffy and pulpy. Once they are soft, add the blackcurrants, and bring to a boil. Simmer, covered, for approximately 2 minutes, or until the fruit is very soft.

Rub the blackcurrant and apple mixture through a nylon sieve in a heatproof bowl set over a pan of simmering hot water. Be sure to keep the heatproof bowl simmering over the pan of hot water and add the sugar to the purée and dissolve. Add the butter and lemon juice once the sugar has dissolved.

Once the butter has melted and the mixture is hot, thick, and glossy, add the beaten egg through a sieve. Stir with a wooden spoon for about 10 minutes, until the curd is thick and creamy (it should coat the back of a spoon). Make sure it doesn't boil or it may curdle. Do not cook for too long, because the curd thickens when cold. Stir in the sloe gin or cassis and immediately pour the curd into sterilized jars. Store in the refrigerator and use within 4 weeks.

Makes approximately 650g (1 lb 7 oz)

raspberry & apple curd

see variations page 93

This is a heavenly spread for buttered toast, brioche, croissants, french toast, and bagels.

225g (8 oz) cooking apples (peeled, cored &
   chopped
3 tbsp. water
1 tbsp. lemon juice
225g (8 oz) raspberries

400g (14 oz) sugar
125g (4½ oz) unsalted butter
1 vanilla pod with seeds removed
4 large eggs, beaten well

Place the chopped apples with the water and lemon juice into a pan and cook until soft, fluffy and pulpy. Once soft, add the raspberries, and bring to a simmering boil. Simmer, covered, for approximately 2 minutes, or until very soft and the juices are running.

Rub the raspberry and apple mixture through a nylon sieve in a heatproof bowl placed over a pan of simmering hot water. Be sure to keep the heatproof bowl simmering over the pan of hot water; add the sugar to the purée and stir to dissolve. Add the butter and vanilla pod seeds once the sugar has dissolved.

Once the butter has melted and the mixture is hot, thick, and glossy, add the beaten egg through a sieve. Stir with a wooden spoon for about 10 minutes, until the curd is thick and creamy (it should coat the back of a spoon). Make sure it doesn't boil or it may curdle. Do not cook for too long, because the curd thickens when cold. Immediately pour the curd into sterilized jars. Store in the refrigerator and use within 4 weeks.

Makes approximately 650g (1 lb 7 oz)

luscious limoncello curd

see variations page 94

This is a firm favourite in my household — it's a great topping for pancakes and waffles.

200ml (7 fl. oz) lemon juice
finely grated zest from 2–3 lemons
125g (4½ oz) unsalted butter

400g (14 oz) sugar
4 large eggs, beaten well
3 tbsp. limoncello

Place the lemon juice, lemon zest, butter, and sugar in a heatproof bowl placed over a pan of simmering water.

Once the butter has melted and the mixture is hot, thick, and glossy, add the beaten egg through a sieve. Stir with a wooden spoon for about 10 minutes, until the curd is thick and creamy (it should coat the back of a spoon). Make sure it doesn't boil or it may curdle. Do not cook for too long, because the curd thickens when cold.

Stir in the limoncello and immediately pour the curd into sterilized jars. Store in the refrigerator and use within 4 weeks.

Makes approximately 650g (1 lb 7 oz)

clippy's classic lime & lemon curd

see variations page 95

I've combined my mum's recipe with a touch of lime to give it more oomph!
Fantastic mixed with a couple of tablespoons of rum blanco and then drizzled over
coconut ice cream.

200ml (7 fl. oz) lemon juice
finely grated zest from 2–3 lemons
200ml (7 fl. oz) lime juice
finely grated zest from 3 limes

125g (4½ oz) unsalted butter
400g (14 oz) sugar
4 large eggs, beaten well

Place the lemon and lime juice and zest, butter, and sugar in a heatproof bowl placed over a
pan of simmering water.

Once the butter has melted and the mixture is hot, thick, and glossy, add the beaten egg
through a sieve. Stir with a wooden spoon for about 10 minutes, until the curd is thick and
creamy (it should coat the back of a spoon). Make sure it doesn't boil or it may curdle. Do
not cook for too long, because the curd thickens when cold.

Immediately pour the curd into sterilized jars. Store in the refrigerator and use within
4 weeks.

Makes approximately 650g (1 lb 7 oz)

orange & orange liqueur curd (reduced sugar and eggs)

see variations page 96

I've reduced the amount of sugar and eggs in this curd. It's not as rich as the previous curds, but the orange liqueur really gives it a lovely warm glow.

juice and zest of 3 large oranges
1½ tbsp. lemon juice
125g (4½ oz) unsalted butter

200g (7 oz) sugar
2 large eggs, beaten well
3 tbsp. orange liqueur

Place the orange, and lemon juice, orange zest, butter, and sugar in a heatproof bowl placed over a pan of simmering water.

Once the butter has melted and the mixture is hot, thick, and glossy, add the beaten egg through a sieve. Stir with a wooden spoon for about 10 minutes, until the curd is thick and creamy (it should coat the back of a spoon). Make sure it doesn't boil or it may curdle. Do not cook for too long, because the curd thickens when cold.

Stir in the orange liqueur. Immediately pour the curd into sterilized jars. Place in the refrigerator and use within 2 weeks.

Makes 450g (1 lb)

egg-free spiced pumpkin curd

see variations page 97

Without the eggs, this is like a spiced pumpkin butter. Excellent for a weekend breakfast.

1kg (2 lbs 4 oz) pumpkin or squash (chopped but unpeeled)
100ml (3½ fl. oz) water
juice and zest of 3 large lemons
125g (4½ oz) butter

½ tsp. cinnamon
¼ tsp. ground allspice
¼ tsp. ground cloves
¼ tsp. ground ginger
1kg (2 lbs 4 oz) light brown muscovado sugar

Simmer the pumpkin in the water until soft to touch, approximately 20 minutes. Remove from the water, peel off the skin, and mash until quite smooth. Don't over-process the pumpkin, because it can get really sticky.

Place the pureed pumpkin, lemon juice, lemon zest, butter, spices, and sugar in a heatproof bowl placed over a pan of simmering water.

Once the butter has melted, and the mixture is hot, thick, and glossy, stir with a wooden spoon until the curd is thick and creamy (it should coat the back of a spoon — approximately 10–20 minutes). Do not let it boil, or it may curdle. Do not cook for too long, because the curd thickens when it's cold.

Immediately pour the curd into sterilized jars. Store in the refrigerator for up to 4 weeks.

Makes 2kg (4 lbs 4 oz)

cranberry curd

see variations page 98

This curd has a fabulous colour. It's deep red and goes well with croissants or spiced raisin rolls with lots of butter and a very strong coffee.

150g (5½ oz) cooking apples (chopped)
300g (10½ oz) cranberries
125g (4½ oz) unsalted butter

zest of 1 large orange
450g (9 oz) light brown muscovado sugar
4 large eggs, beaten well

Place the chopped apples and cranberries with the water into a pan. Keep the lid on because the cranberries are likely to pop, and cook until soft, fluffy, and pulpy.

Rub the cranberry and apple mixture through a nylon sieve in a heatproof bowl placed over a pan of simmering hot water (also known as bain-marie). Add the butter, orange zest, and sugar in a heatproof bowl placed over a pan of simmering water.

Once the butter has melted and the mixture is hot, thick, and glossy, add the beaten egg through a sieve. Stir with a wooden spoon for about 10 minutes, until the curd is thick and creamy (it should coat the back of a spoon). Make sure it doesn't boil or it may curdle. Do not cook for too long, because the curd thickens when cold. Immediately pour the curd into sterilized jars. Place in the refrigerator and use within 4 weeks.

Makes 900g (2 lbs)

four-fruit curd

see variations page 99

I've combined my favourite fruits into this voluptuous curd. Be warned that it's not for the faint-hearted!

150g (5½ oz) passion fruit (pulp only)
115g (4 oz) mango (skin removed)
3 tbsp. water
450g (1 lb) sugar

150g (5½ oz) unsalted butter
juice and zest of 2 medium lemons
juice and zest of 3 limes
4 large eggs, beaten well

Place the passion fruit, mango, and water into a pan and cook until soft. Rub the passion fruit and mango mixture through a sieve in a heatproof bowl placed over a pan of simmering hot water (also known as bain-marie). Be sure to keep the heatproof bowl simmering over the pan of hot water and add the sugar to the purée and stir to dissolve. Add the butter and lemon and lime juice along with the lemon and lime zest.

Once the butter has melted (make sure the mixture is hot, thick, and glossy), add the beaten egg through a sieve, and stir with a wooden spoon until the curd is thick and creamy (it should coat the back of a spoon – approximately 10 minutes). Do not let it boil, or it may curdle. Do not cook for too long, because the curd thickens when it's cold. Immediately pour the curd into sterilized jars. Place in the refrigerator and use within 4 weeks.

Makes approximately 650g (1 lb 7 oz)

spiced apple butter

see variations page 100

A Belgian classic, apple butter is sometimes known as apple cheese. It doesn't contain any dairy at all! This version is light and fresh, but you can cook it for a little longer, until the butter turns a rich brown, for a more traditional, caramelly butter.

1.5kg (3 lbs 5 oz) cooking apples (quartered and chopped)
1 cinnamon stick
5 cloves
5 tbsp. water
450g (1 lb) sugar

Quarter the apples (don't peel or remove the seeds) add to the pan with the cinnamon stick, cloves, and water. Bring to a gentle simmer and cook, partially covered, until it becomes a thick pulp (approximately 30 minutes).

Rub the fruit through a nylon sieve into a large bowl. Stir the pulp with a wooden spoon to help it through the sieve. Discard the seeds, skin, peel, cinnamon stick, and cloves.

Measure the fruit purée into a pan. Add 450g (1 lb) of sugar per 600ml (1 pint) of purée and heat very gently until the sugar dissolves. Bring to a gentle simmer and boil steadily, stirring regularly. This can burn really easily, so watch it carefully. It's ready when a wooden spoon leaves a clear wake (approximately 30 minutes). Remove from the heat. Make sure you grease your containers so that you can remove the butter easily. Spoon into hot sterilized glass containers and seal.

Makes approximately 750g (1 lb 10 oz)

blackberry, apple & lemon cheese

see variations page 101

The combination of apples & blackberries makes this a perfect preserve to enjoy with roast game, sausages, cheeses, and cured meats. Try serving alongside cracked walnuts and squares of dark chocolate.

1kg (2 lbs 4 oz) cooking apples (quartered and chopped)
500g (1 lb 2 oz) blackberries
4 tbsp. water

450g (1 lb) sugar
seeds from 1 vanilla pod
zest of 1 large lemon

Quarter the apples (don't peel or remove the seeds) and add them to the pan along with the blackberries and water. Bring to a gentle simmer and cook, partially covered, until a thick pulp (approximately 30 minutes).

Rub the fruit through a sieve into a large bowl. Stir the pulp with a wooden spoon to help it through the sieve. Discard the seeds, skin, and peel.

Measure the fruit purée into a pan. Add the correct amount of sugar (400g (14 oz) of sugar per 600ml (1 pint) of purée) and heat very gently until the sugar dissolves. Add the vanilla seeds and lemon zest. Bring to a gentle simmer and boil steadily, stirring regularly. This can burn really easily, so don't leave it. It's ready when a wooden spoon leaves a clear wake (approximately 30 minutes). Remove from the heat. Make sure you grease your containers so you can remove the cheese easily. Spoon the cheese into hot sterilized glass containers and seal.

Makes approximately 750g (1 lb 10 oz)

blackcurrant & sloe gin curd

see base recipe page 75

apple, blackberry & cassis curd
Replace the blackcurrants with 225g (8 oz) of blackberries.

apple & orange curd
Replace the blackcurrants with the same amount of juice and zest; omit the sloe gin.

good times apple & mango curd
Replace the blackcurrants with mango. At the end of cooking, grate a dusting of nutmeg and stir; pot the curd. Omit the sloe gin.

apple & lime curd
Replace the blackcurrants with 225g (8 oz) lime zest and juice. Omit the sloe gin.

apple & vanilla curd
Add the seeds from one vanilla pod when melting the butter and sugar.

raspberry & apple curd

see base recipe page 77

zesty appleberry curd
Use the zest from 1 orange and add it at the final stage of cooking, along with the juice from the orange. Omit the vanilla.

apple & quince curd
Replace the raspberries with an equal quantity of quince. Add the zest from 1 lemon when melting the sugar and butter.

raspberry curd
Replace the apples with raspberries and add 2 tablespoons of rose water when cooking the curd.

cinnamon appletastic curd
Omit the raspberries, and vanilla pod; and add 1 teaspoon ground cinnamon when melting the sugar and butter.

apple Calvados curd
Omit the raspberries and replace with extra apples. Add 2 tablespoons of Calvados or apple brandy just before potting.

luscious limoncello curd

see base recipe page 78

lighter limoncello curd
Use only half the butter and proceed as main recipe. It won't last as long as
a regular curd, but maybe that's a good thing!

orgasmic orangecello curd
Replace the lemon juice and zest with orange juice and zest; add orange
liqueur at the end of cooking.

lemony lavender curd
Add 1 tablespoon lavender when heating the juice and zest. Omit the
limoncello.

lemon & cardamom curd
Add 1 teaspoon ground cardamom when melting the butter and sugar. Omit
the limoncello.

lemon posset curd
Proceed as main recipe. Add a couple of tablespoons double cream and
spoon into cool, sterilized jars. This will only keep for about a week.

clippy's classic lime & lemon curd

see base recipe page 81

honey lemon curd
Add 3 tablespoons flavoured honey, such as heather honey, when adding the butter.

lemon and banana curd
Add 2 large bananas, chopped, with the lemon zest and juice at the beginning. Mash the bananas if they do not break down when cooking.

lemon & coconut curd
Add 4 tablespoons coconut milk at the beginning.

blueberry lemon curd
Halve the amount of lemon zest and juice; replace them with blueberries. Cook the blueberries with the sugar, zest, and juice for 5 minutes, until the blueberries are soft. Transfer the blueberries to a blender and purée. Follow the recipe as normal without the sugar.

variations

orange & orange liqueur curd

see base recipe page 82

orange & cardamom curd
Add 1 teaspoon ground cardamom when melting the butter and sugar.

seville orange curd
Replace the navel oranges with Seville oranges and proceed as main recipe.

passion fruit & orange curd
Replace half the oranges with passion fruit. First gently heat the passion fruit purée in a pan and release the seeds from the sticky zingy substance; then continue as per the recipe.

jaffa orange curd
Use Jaffa oranges instead of navel oranges and omit the liqueur.

egg-free spiced pumpkin curd

see base recipe page 83

maple pumpkin curd
Add 3 tablespoons real maple syrup (not flavoured syrup) when cooking the ingredients together.

cinnabon pumpkin curd
Add an extra teaspoon of cinnamon to the curd, and the seeds from a vanilla pod, along with the other spices.

chocolate & pumpkin curd
Melt a handful of chopped, good-quality, dark chocolate when adding the butter and sugar.

velvety vanilla pumpkin curd
Omit the spices and replace with the seeds from 1 vanilla pod; add the seeds at the same time as the sugar and butter.

variations

cranberry curd

see base recipe page 84

spiced cranberry curd
Add 2 tablespoons chopped preserved ginger to the curd before potting.

cherry ginger curd
Replace the cranberries with cherries and proceed as main recipe.

amaretto cherry curd
Replace the cranberries with cherries; add 3 tablespoons of amaretto just before potting. Omit the ground ginger.

clafoutis curd
Replace the cranberries and apples with sweet cherries; add 1 tablespoon vanilla extract when melting the sugar and butter; add 2 tablespoons Kirsch just before potting.

cranberry delight
Replace the apples with cranberries; add the orange juice orange along with the orange zest.

variations

four-fruit curd

see base recipe page 87

citrus, passion fruit & mango curd
Replace the lime with 2 oranges (juice and zest); proceed as main recipe.

passion fruit curd
Replace all the fruit with passion fruit. Gently heat the passion fruit purée in a pan to release the seeds and then continue as per the recipe.

strawberry & lemon curd
Replace the mango and passion fruit with strawberries and omit the limes; replace the limes with lemons.

fruity ginger curd
Add 2 teaspoons freshly grated ginger when melting the butter and sugar.

variations

spiced apple cheese

see base recipe page 88

calvados apple cheese
In the final stage of cooking add 2 tablespoons of Calvados (apple brandy).

spiced apple & pear cheese
Replace half the apples with pears and follow the recipe.

vanilla apple cheese
Omit the spices and add the seeds from 1 vanilla pod.

quince apple cheese
Omit the spices and replace half the apples with quince; follow the recipe.

hot chili apple cheese
Omit the spices and add 1 teaspoon crushed dried chili flakes at the beginning when cooking the apples.

blackberry, apple & lemon cheese

see base recipe page 91

plum, almond & lemon cheese
Replace the blackberries with cooking plums (not dessert plums); replace the lemon zest with 55g (2 oz) flaked roasted almonds and add when the sugar has dissolved. Omit the vanilla.

damson & apple cheese
Replace the blackberries with damsons (seeded); continue with the recipe.

blackcurrant & apple cheese
Replace the blackberries with blackcurrants. Omit the lemon and follow the recipe. Add 1 tablespoon of cassis at the end of cooking before potting.

gooseberry lemon cheese
Replace the blackberries and apples with gooseberries and follow the recipe. Omit the vanilla.

marmalades

This was the first preserve I made at the tender age of ten, and I've never lost the love of the intoxicating smell of cooking marmalade. The whole fruit is used, including the skin, juice, and seeds. Marmalades need longer to cook compared to jams because of the addition of the peel, which needs to be soft before adding the sugar.

seville orange marmalade

see variations page 121

A classic marmalade; the bitter oranges make this a not-too-sweet breakfast treat.

1kg (2 lbs 3 oz) Seville oranges
5½ tbsp. freshly squeezed lemon juice

1.5kg (3 lbs 5 oz)
500g (1 lb 2 oz) brown sugar

First, scrub the oranges and remove the buttons from the top of the fruit. Cut them in half and give them a vigorous squeeze to release the juice. Keep the seeds and place them in a muslin bag. Using a very sharp knife, slice the peel into thin shreds. Then place the freshly squeezed orange juice, muslin bag, and the shredded peel in the bowl, cover, and leave for 24 hours.

Empty the contents of the bowl into a preserving pan. Then slowly bring to a boil, covered, for approximately 2 hours, or until the peel is tender to touch and the mixture has reduced.

Next remove the muslin bag and stir in the lemon juice and both sugars. Once the sugars have dissolved, bring the mixture up to a rolling boil. Be careful when boiling the marmalade because it can spit and burn you. It should take about 20–25 minutes to reach the setting point. Once you have a set, remove from the heat and let it cool for 10 minutes. Then pour into warm, sterilized jars and seal.

Makes 2.2kg (4 lb 13 oz)

grapefruit marmalade

see variations page 122

The tangy bite of grapefruit makes this marmalade a true classic. If you can find the ruby red grapefruit, the colour of this preserve is beautiful.

480g (1 lb 1 oz) grapefruit (ruby red if possible)
1 litre (1¾ pints) water

930g (2 lbs) sugar
3 tbsp. dark spiced rum

In this recipe, the fruit is not shredded beforehand. Instead, the grapefruits are simmered whole until tender. First, scrub the grapefruit and remove the buttons from the top of the fruit. Place them in the water (make sure the pan is deep enough to cover the fruit) and bring to a boil. Simmer, covered, for approximately 2–2½ hours, or until you can pierce the skin easily with a fork or skewer.

Carefully remove the grapefruit from the water and let cool (do not discard the cooking liquid). Once it's cool enough to handle, chop in half. Remove the seeds and squeeze any juice into the remaining liquid. Discard the seeds. Cut the grapefruit into thinly sliced pieces.

Add the sugar, grapefruit liquid, and thinly sliced grapefruit to the pan. Once the sugar has dissolved, bring to a rolling boil. Be careful when boiling the marmalade because it can spit and burn you. It should take about 15 minutes to reach the setting point. Once you have a set, remove from the heat and let cool for 10 minutes. Stir to distribute the peel. Add the dark spiced rum and pour into warm, sterilized jars and seal.

Makes 2.2kg (4 lb 13 oz)

old-fashioned marmalade

see variations page 123

I love this old-fashioned version of marmalade often known as "Oxford Marmalade."

450g (1 lb) Seville oranges
1.25 litres (2 pints) water

900g (2 lbs) brown sugar
3 tbsp. black treacle

In this recipe the fruit is not shredded beforehand. Instead, the oranges are simmered whole until they are lovely and tender. First scrub the oranges and remove the buttons from the top of the fruit. Place them in the water and bring them to a boil. Simmer, covered, for approximately 2–2½ hours, or until you can pierce the skin easily with a fork or skewer.

Carefully remove the oranges from the water and let cool (do not discard the cooking liquid). Once cool enough to handle, chop the oranges in half, remove the seeds, and squeeze any juice into the remaining liquid. Discard the seeds. Cut up the oranges into thick, chunky pieces.

Add the sugar, black black treacle, orange liquid, and the cut up oranges to the pan. Once the sugar has dissolved, bring to a rolling boil. Be careful when boiling the marmalade because it can spit and burn you. It should take about 15 minutes to reach the setting point. Once you have a set, remove from the heat and let cool for 10 minutes. Stir and pour into warm, sterilized jars and seal.

Makes 1.5kg (3 lb 5 oz)

the one-hour marmalade

see variations page 124

Using the whole fruit from the beginning and cooking for only an hour gives a very robust marmalade.

450g (1 lb) navel oranges
750ml (1¼ pints) water
650g (1 lb 7 oz) sugar

Halve the oranges and remove any of the seeds (place the seeds in a muslin bag), and slice the oranges very thinly — if the orange peel is sliced thickly, it will not cook evenly and can become chewy once the sugar is added. Take care to catch all the juice and put in the pan along with all the oranges. Add the water to the pan, along with the muslin bag, and bring the mixture to the boil. Simmer gently, uncovered, for approximately 45 minutes, or until the orange peel is soft and tender. The contents of the pan should be reduced by half.

Once you have checked that the peel is soft and tender, add the sugar gradually, stirring until it is dissolved. Remove the muslin bag. Bring the mixture to a full rolling boil; do not stir the marmalade at this stage because this reduces the heat and the setting point. Test the set after 5 minutes. Marmalade has only a brief period when it is at its setting point, so it is imperative that you test early. Once you pass the setting point, there is no return! Keep testing the set and make sure you take the pan off the heat when doing so.

Once you have a set (either plate or flake test), allow the marmalade to cool for 10 minutes. Then stir to distribute the peel and pour into sterilized jars. Use within 2 years.

Makes 700g (1 lb 8 oz)

spiced orange &
tangerine marmalade

see variations page 125

Using the base of the one-hour marmalade, I've given this marmalade a little twist by adding tangerines, some heat and some apple juice, which works well with tangerines.

300g (10½ oz) navel oranges
4 oz tangerines
375ml (12½ fl. oz) water
375ml (12½ fl. oz) apple juice

650g (1 lb 7 oz) sugar
1 tsp. crushed dried chili flakes
2 tbsp. lemon juice

Halve the oranges and remove any of the seeds (place the seeds in a muslin bag), and slice the oranges and tangerines very thinly — if the orange peel is sliced thickly, it will not cook evenly and can become chewy once the sugar is added. Take care to catch all the juice and put in the pan along with all the oranges and tangerines. Add the water and apple juice to the pan and bring to a boil. Simmer gently, uncovered, for approximately 45 minutes, or until the fruit peel is soft and tender. The contents of the pan should be reduced by half.

Once the peel is soft and tender, add the sugar gradually. Add the lemon juice and chili flakes, stirring until the sugar has dissolved. Bring the mixture to a full rolling boil. Do not stir the marmalade at this stage because it reduces the heat and the setting point. Test the set after 5 minutes. Keep testing the set and make sure you take the pan off the heat when doing so. Once you have a set (either plate or flake test), allow the marmalade to cool for 10 minutes. Then stir to distribute the peel and pour into sterilized jars. Use within 2 years.

Makes 700g (1 lb 8 oz)

aromatic orange marmalade

see variations page 126

The orange flower water adds a light fragrance to this marmalade that can't fail to cheer you up. This preserve is delicious when paired with smooth pâtés and mature cheddar.

450g (1 lb) Seville oranges
1.25 litres (2 pints) water

930g (2 lbs) sugar
2 tbsp. orange flower water

In this recipe the fruit is not shredded beforehand. Instead, the oranges are simmered whole until tender. First scrub the oranges and remove the buttons from the top of the fruit. Place them in the water and bring them to a boil and then simmer, covered, for approximately 2–2½ hours, or until you can pierce the skin easily with a fork or skewer.

Carefully remove the oranges from the water and let them cool (do not discard the cooking liquid). Once cool enough to handle, chop them in half, remove the seeds, and squeeze any juice into the remaining liquid. Then discard the seeds. Cut the oranges into thick, chunky pieces.

Add the sugar, liquid, and chopped oranges to the pan. Once the sugar has dissolved, bring the mixture to a rolling boil. Be careful when boiling the marmalade because it can spit and burn you. It should take about 15 minutes to reach the setting point. Once you have a set, remove from the heat. Add the orange flower water and let cool for 10 minutes. Stir and pour into warm, sterilized jars. Seal.

Makes 1.5kg (3 lb 5 oz)

ginger marmalade

see variations page 127

I love adding ginger to marmalade, and this is one of my top favourites. Try brushing on chicken skewers or sausages before barbecuing.

300g (10½ oz) navel oranges
700ml (1¼ pints) water
650g (1 lb 7 oz) sugar
2 tbsp. lemon juice

175g (6 oz) chopped preserved ginger
50ml (2 fl. oz) ginger syrup (from the preserved
   ginger jar)
1/2 tsp. crushed dried chili flakes

Halve the oranges. Remove any seeds (place the seeds in a muslin bag), and slice the fruit very thinly – if the orange peel is sliced thickly, it will not cook evenly and can become chewy once the sugar is added. Add the water, orange shreds, and the muslin bag to the pan. Take care to catch all the juice and put it in the pan along with the oranges. Bring to a boil and simmer gently, uncovered, for approximately 45 minutes, or until the fruit peel is soft and tender. The contents of the pan should reduce by half.

Once you have checked that the peel is soft and tender, remove the muslin bag and gradually add the sugar, lemon juice, chopped ginger, ginger syrup, and chili flakes, stirring until the sugar has dissolved. Bring the mixture to a full rolling boil. Test the set after 5 minutes. Keep testing the set and make sure you take the pan off the heat when doing so. Once you have a set (either plate or flake test, allow the marmalade to cool for 10 minutes. Stir to distribute the peel and pour into sterilized jars. Use within 2 years.

Makes 700g (1 lb 8 oz)

quince & lemon marmalade

see variations page 128

This recipe is based on my Auntie Andie's quince marmalade. I've given the recipe a twist with apple juice & lemons instead of the more traditional limes.

225g (8 oz) lemons
250ml (9 fl. oz) non-sparkling cider
650g (1 lb 7 oz) ripe quince

500ml (16 fl. oz) water
650g (1 lb 7 oz) sugar

First scrub the lemons and remove the buttons from the top of the fruit. Cut them in half and give them a vigorous squeeze to release the juice. Keep the seeds and place them in a muslin bag. Using a very sharp knife, slice the peel into thin shreds (no pith, because this will make the marmalade bitter). Place half of the freshly squeezed lemon juice, cider, and the shredded peel into the bowl. Cover while you prepare the quince.

Peel and core the quince and put the quince parings in the muslin bag and tighten. Then thinly slice the quince and put it in a bowl with the remaining lemon juice (this will prevent the quince from discolouring).

Place all the ingredients, except for the marinated quince slices and the sugar, in a pot and cook for 20–30 minutes, until soft to the touch. Add the quince mixture and simmer until the quince is soft. Remove the muslin bag and add the sugar. Once it is dissolved, bring the quince mixture to a rolling boil. Once you have a set, let it cool for 10 minutes. Stir to redistribute the quince and spoon into sterilized jars.

Makes 1.1kg (2lb 4 oz)

whiskey & almond marmalade

see variations page 129

This Scottish traditional recipe is how my granny made her marmalade, full of intense flavours. Served with homemade bread and butter, it was my gran's vice and is mine too!

500g (1 lb 2 oz) Seville oranges
1 litre (1¾ pints) water
950g (2 lbs) brown sugar

3 tbsp. whiskey
200g (7 oz) flaked toasted almonds

In this recipe the fruit is not shredded beforehand. Instead, the oranges are simmered whole until they are lovely and tender. First scrub the oranges and remove the buttons from the top of the fruit. Place them in the water and bring to a boil. Then simmer, covered for approximately 2–2½ hours, or until you can pierce the skin easily with a fork or skewer.

Carefully remove the oranges from the water and let cool (do not discard the cooking liquid). Once cool enough to handle, chop the oranges in half, remove the seeds. and squeeze any juice into the remaining liquid. Discard the seeds. Finely cut up the oranges.

Add the sugar, orange liquid and the cut up oranges to the pan. Once the sugar has dissolved, bring the mixture to a rolling boil. Be careful when boiling the marmalade, because it can spit and burn you. It should take about 15 minutes to reach the setting point.

Once you have a set, remove from the heat, add the whiskey and flaked almonds, and let cool for 10 minutes. Stir and pour into warm, sterilized jars. Seal.

Makes 1.5kg (3 lb 5 oz)

marmachili

see variations page 130

For those who like a spicy, firmer-set marmalade, here's the perfect recipe!

500g (1 lb 2 oz) Seville oranges
2½ tbsp. freshly squeezed lemon juice
1 tbsp. crushed chili flakes

1kg (2 lbs 4 oz) sugar
2 tbsp. preserved ginger, finely diced

First scrub the oranges and remove the buttons from the top of the fruit. Cut the oranges in half and give them a vigorous squeeze to release the juice. Keep the seeds and place them in a muslin bag. Using a very sharp knife, slice the peel into thin shreds. Place the freshly squeezed orange juice, muslin bag, and the shredded peel in a bowl. Cover and leave for 24 hours.

Empty the contents of the bowl into a preserving pan. Slowly bring to a boil, covered, for approximately 2 hours, or until the peel is tender to the touch and the mixture has reduced.

Remove the muslin bag and stir in the lemon juice, sugar, chili flakes, and diced ginger. Once the sugar has dissolved, bring the mixture to a rolling boil. Be careful when boiling, because the marmalade can spit and burn you. It should take about 15 minutes to reach the setting point. Once you have a set, remove from the heat and let cool for 10 minutes. Pour into warm, sterilized jars and seal.

Makes 1.1kg (2lb 4 oz)

four-fruit marmalade

see variations page 131

This tangy preserve is perfect for breakfast served with toast and English muffins. Also a match made in heaven with a coarse pâté or hand-carved ham.

1 medium grapefruit
1 large orange (sweet)
2 medium Seville oranges
2 medium limes

1.5 litres (2^1/$_3$ pints) water
1 tbsp. coriander seeds
3 tbsp. lemon juice
1.2kg (2 lbs 5 oz) light muscovado sugar

First scrub the fruit and remove the buttons from the top of the fruit. Cut the fruit in half and give them a vigorous squeeze to release the juice. Keep the seeds and place them in a muslin bag. Using a very sharp knife, slice the peel into thin shreds. Dry roast the coriander seeds and then crush in a pestle and mortar and add to the muslin bag. Place the squeezed fruit juices, muslin bag, and the shredded peel in the bowl. Cover and leave for 24 hours.

Empty the contents of the bowl into a preserving pan with the water. Slowly bring the fruit to a boil, covered for approximately 2 hours, or until the peel is tender to the touch. You'll also notice that the marmalade mixture will have reduced.

Remove the muslin bag and stir in the lemon juice and the light brown muscovado sugar. Once the sugar has dissolved, bring the mixture to a rolling boil. Be careful when boiling the marmalade, because it can spit and burn you. It should take about 20–25 minutes to reach the setting point. Once you have a set, remove from the heat and let cool for 10 minutes. Pour into warm, sterilized jars and seal.

Makes 1.3kg (2lb 11 oz)

variations

seville orange marmalade

see base recipe page 103

tickle-your-taste-buds marmalade
Replace the brown sugar with caster sugar. Then add 2 tablespoons of a robust orange flavoured vodka just before you pot the marmalade.

seville & kumquat marmalade
Replace a quarter of the Seville oranges with kumquats (thinly sliced) and proceed as main recipe.

seville orangeade marmalade
Add 4 tablespoons of dry, sparking white wine when the marmalade is ready to pot.

seville & carrot marmalade
Replace a quarter of the Seville oranges with grated carrots. Continue with the recipe.

variations

grapefruit marmalade

see base recipe page 105

minted grapefruit marmalade
Replace the dark spiced rum with 3 tablespoons freshly chopped mint.
Add the mint when you've reached the setting point.

christmas cranberry marmalade
Add 140g (5 oz) fresh cranberries to the grapefruit.

honey grapefruit marmalade
Omit the rum and replace with robust honey.

grapefruit cardamom marmalade
Bruise 10 cardamom pods and place them in a muslin bag. Place the
whole grapefruit in the bag. When you add the sugar, squeeze the bag
to make sure you get a nice cardamom syrup; add it to the marmalade.
Omit the rum.

star anise grapefruit marmalade
Add 2 star anise to the whole grapefruit while cooking. Remove the star
anise when you add the sugar. When you pot the marmalade, add 1 star
anise to the marmalade. Omit the rum.

old-fashioned marmalade

see base recipe page 106

cardamom orange marmalade
Add a spoonful of crushed cardamom pods at the beginning when you cook the oranges.

orange & apricot nectar marmalade
Omit the black black treacle and replace it with honey. Halve the amount of Seville oranges; add dried whole unsulfured apricots. Cook with the whole oranges. Replace the sugar with granulated sugar.

ottoman marmalade
Add 10 cloves to the Seville oranges so they impart their flavour; replace the black black treacle with 3 tablespoons rose water. Add the rose water at the end cooking.

rum & raisin marmalade
Omit the black black treacle and add 3 tablespoons of raisins along with the sugar. Add 1 tablespoon dark rum to the sterilized jar; pour in the marmalade.

variations

the one-hour marmalade

see base recipe page 109

muscovado marmalade
Use half light brown muscovado sugar and half dark brown muscovado sugar; this will produce a darker marmalade.

sunshine fruits marmalade
Replace half the oranges with lemons and continue with the recipe.

gingered orange marmalade
Add 2 tablespoons freshly grated ginger in the final stage of cooking.

miss sassy marmalade
Add 3 tablespoons of orange vodka or marmalade vodka just before potting.

spiced orange & tangerine marmalade

see base recipe page 110

brandied marmalade
Add 2 tablespoons of apple brandy just before you pot the marmalade.

lip-smacking cinnamon marmalade
Add 1 cinnamon stick to the citrus fruit but remove when potting. Omit the chili flakes.

orange vanilla marmalade
Replace the granulated sugar with vanilla infused sugar and omit the chili flakes.

tangy marmalade
Give this marmalade an extra boost. Replace half the oranges with blood oranges and continue with the recipe.

variations

chunky seville orange marmalade

see base recipe page 111

nutty seville marmalade
Replace the orange flower water and add 85g (3 oz) toasted chopped hazelnuts, once you've reached setting point. Cool for ten minutes, then stir before potting.

granny green's dundee marmalade
Add 1 tablespoon of whisky (preferably a single malt) to each sterilized jar and then pour in the marmalade. Omit the orange blossom water.

robust seville marmalade
Replace the sugars with dark brown sugar for a darker robust marmalade.

grapefruit & seville orange marmalade
Replace half the Seville oranges with grapefruit and prepare the same way. Omit the orange flower water.

ginger marmalade

see base recipe page 113

ginger wine marmalade
Add 3 tablespoons of ginger wine to the final stage of cooking, just before potting the marmalade.

ultimate ginger marmalade
Omit the chili flakes. Add 2 tablespoons freshly grated ginger with the stem ginger and ginger syrup.

lemon ginger marmalade
Replace the oranges with lemons; follow the recipe. Remove the chili flakes and add 1 tablespoon fresh red chili (finely sliced).

the hot toddy marmalade
Omit the chilies and add 1 lemon sliced, and the juice, at the beginning of the recipe.

lime ginger marmalade
Replace the oranges with limes and follow the recipe.

variations

quince & lemon marmalade

see base recipe page 114

quince & vanilla marmalade
Replace the cider with apple juice. Add the seeds from the 1 vanilla pod; omit the lemon.

quince & lime marmalade
Replace the lemon with a lime and replace the cider with apple juice; follow the recipe.

ginger quince marmalade
Add 3 tablespoons crystalized ginger just before potting.

ruby quince marmalade
Use red quince, and add an extra lemon for added zing.

quince geranium marmalade
Add a handful of pesticide-free geranium leaves with the quince. Remove the leaves before potting.

quince rose water marmalade
Replace the water with apple juice. Add 3 tablespoons rose water just before potting.

whiskey & almond marmalade

see base recipe page 117

golden marmalade
Replace the brown sugar with granulated sugar; replace half the Seville oranges with a mix of tangerines and clementines. Proceed as main recipe. Swap the whiskey for an almond liqueur.

tipsy marmalade
Replace the brown sugar with light brown sugar; replace the whiskey with 1 tablespoon each of Campari, gin, and orange bitters

chocolate–orange marmalade
Omit the whiskey. Replace with 3 tablespoons freshly grated dark chocolate added to the marmalade just before potting.

orange & licorice marmalade
Omit the whiskey and almond. Add 2 sticks of sweet chewy licorice when cooking the oranges. Then follow the recipe.

variations

marmachili

see base recipe page 118

mixed-spice marmalade
Replace the chili with mixed spice; add at the beginning of cooking.

saffron-infused marmalade
Omit the chili flakes and ginger; replace with a large pinch saffron threads and follow the recipe.

orange nutmeg marmalade
Omit the ginger and chili; replace with ½ teaspoon ground nutmeg and the seeds from 1 vanilla pod. Proceed as main recipe.

blood orange marmalade
Replace the navel oranges with blood oranges and proceed as main recipe.

maple marmalade
Omit the ginger and chili; replace with 6 tablespoons pure maple syrup and 1 cinnamon stick. Proceed with the recipe.

variations

four-fruit marmalade

see base recipe page 120

rum & raisin fruit marmalade
Replace the coriander seeds and add 85g (3 oz) raisins to the first cook before adding the sugar. Add 2 tablespoons of rum just before you pot the marmalade.

schezuan pepper marmalade
Omit the coriander seeds and add 1 teaspoon freshly ground Szechuan pepper.

pistachio four-fruit marmalade
Omit the coriander seeds and replace with 2 tablespoons roasted chopped pistachios; add at the end of cooking just before potting.

fruity marmalade
Replace the large orange with 2 lemons; follow the recipe.

liqueurs

The essence of summer packed and ready for a dark

winter's night! Some tips: Use alcohol with at least

40 per cent alcohol; the sugar needs to be white or

light golden in order to get the best result; and the

fruit must be in perfect condition (i.e., fresh, top

quality, and not underripe).

spiced vanilla vodka

see variations page 148

Simply heaven. Keep the vodka in the freezer, for a cold but warming tipple.

1 blade of mace
2.5-cm (1-in.) chunk of fresh ginger
½ cinnamon stick
3 tbsp. brandy

2 vanilla pods
200–300ml (7–10 fl. oz) vodka (at least 40%
  alcohol)

Wrap the mace, ginger, and cinnamon in a muslin bag, and place in a small saucepan with the brandy. Gently simmer for 10–15 minutes. Let steep for 20 minutes to infuse the spice flavours into the brandy after simmering.

Place the vanilla pods in the bottle (whole). Then add the infused brandy (but not the spice bag) and add enough vodka to fill the bottle. Seal. Set aside for 2–3 months to let the vanilla and spices develop. It will turn a chocolate-brown colour. Serve chilled over ice or add a couple of glugs to a glass of prosecco. Use within 2 years.

Makes 1 small bottle

plum brandy

see variations page 149

My friend Alex's plum brandy is legendary. He would never tell me his recipe, so I've come up with my own. Perfect in cocktails, on its own, or used in baking.

500g (1 lb 2 oz) plums
500g (1 lb 2 oz) caster sugar or baker's sugar
1 litre (1¾ pints) brandy

First wash and dry the plums. Then pierce the skins and place them in a large Kilner jar. Then add the sugar and cover with brandy. Seal and shake gently to disperse the sugar. Leave the jar somewhere where you can see it, because you'll need to shake the jar regularly over the following weeks.

Every day for the next couple of weeks take the jar and shake it until the sugar dissolves. Once dissolved, leave the jar in a cool, dark place for approximately 2–3 months. Strain the plum brandy through a sieve, so that you have a vibrant, plum-coloured brandy. Decant and let the brandy mature. This makes a perfect festive aperitif.

Makes approximately 1 litre (1¾ pints)

crème de cassis

see variations page 150

The trick is to use really good quality red wine when making cassis liqueur, one that has just been opened. The best wines are fruity ones such as Merlot.

1.5kg (3 lb 5 oz) blackcurrants
2 litres (2½ pints) good-quality wine

1.7kg (2 lbs 12 oz) sugar
100ml (3½ fl. oz) vodka

First remove the tufty tops of the blackcurrants and wash them. Dry and place them in a large pan. Give them a gentle crush with a potato masher, until all the lovely purple juice runs from the fruit.

Pour the fruity red wine over the blackcurrants, give them a good stir, and let marinate for 48 hours. Give them a good stir from time to time, because this will ensure that all the goodness of the heady fruity mix will give you an excellent base for the liqueur.

Transfer the mixture to a jelly bag and strain the fruit mix overnight. The next morning, wash out the pan. Add the juice and sugar to the pan; heat until the sugar is dissolved. For the next hour or so, reduce the liquid until it becomes thick and syrupy. The liquid must not boil, but keep it at a steady simmer.

Let the liquid cool, add in the vodka, and stir to distribute. Pour into sterilized bottles. Allow to mature for several months. Once opened, use within 2 years.

Makes approximately 2 litres (2½ pints)

sloe gin

see variations page 151

We used to forage the blackthorn bushes every summer and bring home the bounty, and my dad would turn them into alcoholic concoctions. Sloe gin is the perfect after-dinner drink.

1kg (2 lbs 3 oz) sloes
1.1kg (2 lbs 6 oz) sugar (or less, if preferred)
1.3 litres (2¼ pints) gin

First wash the sloes and prick them all over with a skewer, or leave them in the freezer overnight. The skins will split open. Place the sloes in a large clear bottle and add the sugar and gin. Shake to get the sloe juice flowing.

Shake the mixture on a daily basis for the next 10 days to 2 weeks; this will prevent the sugar from resting on the bottom of the jar. After this time, leave the jar somewhere cool and dark for 10 weeks. Shake the jar once a week to enhance the flavour.

Once the sloes have imparted their flavour, pass the mixture through a fine sieve. Pour the liqueur into sterilized bottles. Let the bottles mature for 2 years . It's worthwhile making this each year, so you always have a bottle to enjoy.

Don't waste the sloes; remove the stones and try adding the fruit to ice cream. You could also add the fruit to a cupcake batter for an inspired (adult!) sloe gin cupcake. Or dip the sloes in chocolate for a berry treat.

Makes approximately 2 litres (2½ pints)

elderflower champagne

see variations page 152

Elderflower Champagne won't start fermenting until it's under pressure. Make sure you pick the flowers when it's dry out and at the end of the day when the natural yeast is at its best. You should only use bottles meant for brewing purposes.

3 lemons (juiced and zested)
800g (1 lb 10 oz) sugar
4 litres (7 pints) hot water

15 large elderflower heads (in full bloom)
2 tbsp. white wine vinegar

First zest and juice the lemons. Dissolve the sugar in a large pan, then add the water. Add the elderflower heads, juice of the lemons, zest, and the vinegar. When the water temperature is about 104°F, remove from the heat and stir. Use something to weigh down the flowers so that they don't get mouldy (like a ceramic plate). Cover the pan loosely with a clean muslin for up to 48 hours; you should notice that there is a slight foam on top of the brew. If not, add a pinch of yeast to help speed up the fermentation process. After a day or so you should see a small brown patch develop; if so, you're onto a winner (it's the yeast working).

Let the brew ferment for a few days (approximately 3–4 days) before straining and bottling into strong sterilized bottles fitted with hinged stoppers or screw-top bottles. A great deal of pressure builds up inside the bottle from the release of carbon dioxide, so it's important to use the correct bottle. Open and close the bottles every day for a week, so that you can let some of the air out. Store and let ferment for at least a week. Serve chilled. Warning: Be careful when opening the bottles because a great deal of pressure builds up inside them!

Makes approximately 6 litres (10 pints)

citrus vodka

see variations page 153

This is a classic alcoholic tipple to try at home, and it tastes sublime. It's perfect for a summer night sitting in the garden. Enjoy with a few spiced nuts.

3 large lemons
1 small lime
400ml (14 fl. oz) neutral-flavoured vodka

Wash and scrub the lemons to remove the wax. Quarter the lemons and lime and place in a large Kilner jar. Pour the vodka over the lemons and limes and let it infuse for a week in a cool, dark place.

Taste for flavour in one week. If you want a real kick of citrus fruit, let it infuse for approximately 3 weeks. Strain and discard the citrus fruits and pour the vodka into the bottle. Enjoy ice cold or as a shot from the freezer.

Makes 1 small bottle

blood orange liqueur

see variations page 154

You can't beat making your own orange liqueur; it's lusciously tongue tingling. Try to use grain spirit with a high alcohol content, because this will help draw out the orange oil from the peel. Serve as an aperitif or add to crêpes suzette.

1.4kg (3 lb) blood oranges	200g (14 oz) sugar
600ml (1 pint) grain spirit or vodka	600ml (1 pint) water

First scrub the oranges and then carefully peel them so that you have the peel and no pith attached (the white pith will make the liqueur bitter).

Place the peel in a large glass container (preferably a Kilner jar, because you'll need to seal the peel and spirit/vodka for at least a week). Pour the spirit/vodka over the peel, seal the jar, and let infuse for a week in a cool, dark cupboard.

After a week, heat the sugar and water in a pan over a low heat, until the sugar has dissolved. Let cool. Strain into a container, and then add the cooled sugar syrup. Decant into bottles with screw tops or stoppers. Store in the freezer and enjoy responsibly!

Makes approximately 1.5 litres (2¾ pints)

cherry ratafia

see variations page 155

Ideas for my recipes come from my travels around the world. While living in and working in the south of France, I came across this truly delicious alcoholic beverage.

1 vanilla pod
600g (1 lb 5 oz) cherries (pitted)
600ml (1 pint) good quality brandy

1 cinnamon stick
250ml (9 fl. oz) water
250g (9 oz) sugar

Split the vanilla bean pod and add it to a container large enough to hold all the ingredients, except the sugar and water. Add the pitted cherries, brandy, and cinnamon; seal. Let this mixture macerate for 6 weeks, shaking it gently every few days. Strain.

Bring the water and sugar to a gentle boil and simmer until the sugar has dissolved. Add this to the cherry liqueur, stirring all the juiciness together. Transfer to sterilized bottles and store in a dry, cool place. Leave to mature for six months.

Don't forget that the cherries will be full of cinnamon and vanilla goodness, so try adding them to mascarpone for an Italian-style summer pudding. Or they're delicious dipped in dark chocolate.

Makes 1.1 litres (2 pints)

variations

spiced vanilla vodka

see base recipe page 133

spiced vanilla rum
Replace the vodka with white rum.

spiced vanilla brandy
Replace the vodka with brandy.

rose & vanilla vodka
Add 2 packages of dried rose petals to the vodka; omit the spice mix and brandy.

thai-spiced vodka
Omit the brandy, spices, and vanilla; replace with 5 sticks lemongrass, 2 dried red chilies, and a dab of ginger (sliced). Set aside to infuse.

juniper berry vodka
Replace all the ingredients, except the vodka; add 2 tablespoons juniper berries.

variations

plum brandy

see base recipe page 135

plum vodka
Use half vodka and half brandy.

williams pear brandy
Replace the plums with pears.

Calvados (apple brandy)
Replace the plums with apples; add 1 cinnamon stick.

spiced apricot brandy
Replace the plums with fresh apricots; add 1 cinnamon stick, 1 vanilla pod, and 5 cardamom pods.

peach nectarine brandy
Replace the plums with half peaches and half nectarines.

quince brandy
Replace the plums with quince; add 1 teaspoon lavender at the beginning of the recipe.

variations

crème de cassis

see base recipe page 136

blackcurrant vodka
Replace the red wine with vodka.

cranberry vodka
Replace the blackcurrants with cranberries; add the zest from 1 orange.

raspberry liqueur
Replace the blackcurrants with raspberries; add 3 tablespoons of rose water at the end.

soft fruit liqueur
Use a combination of your favourite soft fruits and follow the recipe.

passion fruit liqueur
Replace the blackcurrants with the seeds from the passion fruit; omit the red wine and use white wine instead.

strawberry liqueur
Replace the blackcurrants with strawberries; add the seeds from one vanilla pod.

variations

sloe gin

see base recipe page 139

damson gin
Replace the sloes with damsons, reduce the sugar to 2 cups.

victoria plum gin
Replace the sloes with Victoria plums.

spiced winter gin
Add 1 cinnamon stick, 10 allspice berries, 10 cloves, 1 dab of ginger (sliced), and the rind from 1 orange to the sloes, gin and sugar.

currant gin
Replace the sloes with blackcurrants, redcurrants and white currants (equal amounts).

elderberry gin
Replace the sloes with elderberries (remove the stalks); add 2 vanilla pods.

variations

elderflower champagne

see base recipe page 140

elderflower orange champagne
Replace 1 lemon with an orange; use the juice and zest from the orange as per the recipe.

elderflower rose champagne
Add 1 package of dried rose petals with the elderflowers.

spiced elderflower champagne
Add 1 dab of freshly grated ginger with the flower heads.

infused lavender champagne
Add 3 teaspoons dried lavender to the elderflower heads.

minty elderflower champagne
Add 5 sprigs of fresh mint with the elderflowers.

citrus vodka

see base recipe page 143

spiced orange vodka
Swap the lemons for the oranges; add 1 tablespoon crushed cardamom pods when infusing the vodka with the oranges and limes.

cranorange vodka
Replace half the limes with cranberries.

zingy vodka
Replace 2 lemons with 1 grapefruit; follow the recipe.

red chili vodka
Replace the fruit with 5 dried chilies; set aside to infuse. Keep the chilies for added colour.

mint vodka
Replace the fruit with 10 sprigs of mint.

variations

orange liqueur

see base recipe page 144

orange cinnamon
Add a cinnamon stick at the beginning when infusing the alcohol; discard it with the orange peelings.

orange cardamom
Add 1 tablespoon crushed cardamom pods with the orange peel.

st clements liqueur
Replace half the oranges with lemons and limes.

orange & vanilla
Add 2 spilt vanilla pods with the orange peelings.

spiced orange liqueur
1 cinnamon stick, 1 dab freshly sliced ginger, 1 teaspoon cloves, 1 teaspoon allspice berries; add with the orange peelings.

orangecello
Replace blood oranges with navel oranges.

variations

clippy's cherry ratafia

see base recipe page 147

cherry blast
Replace the brandy with vodka; follow the same recipe.

cherry bakewell
Omit the cinnamon and replace with 2 tablespoons almond extract.

cherry liqueur
Omit the spices and follow the recipe.

spiced cherry liqueur
Add 2 cinnamon sticks.

sour cherry
Replace the cherries with sour cherries for a more robust flavour.

bottled fruits

Bottled fruits are simply submerged in alcohol and sprinkled with sugar, so they can be stored for months. The most famous of all is the Rumtopf — a mixture of summer fruits layered with rum/brandy and sugar, which is stored over the summer in a sealed container ready to enjoy at Christmas. Pretty as a picture, and completely delicious.

drunken raspberries

see variations page 165

I couldn't get through the summer without this jar of goodies sitting in my cupboard. Serve with pancakes, waffles with big scoops of ice cream, or eat straight from the jar.

3/4 cup sugar
3 cups water
2 lbs 3 oz raspberries (hulled)

1/2 cup vodka
5 tbsp. rose syrup or water

Make a sugar syrup — put the sugar and water in a pan and bring to a boil, just until the sugar dissolves. Place the raspberries in warm, sterilized jars, packing them quite tightly. Pour the vodka and rose syrup over the raspberries, then fill the jars with the sugar syrup. Put the lids on the jars, turning only half way — this will help the steam escape.

Place the jars in a pan and cover up to the shoulder of the jar with warm water. Gently heat the water to a simmer and simmer for 25 minutes. Remove the hot jars carefully and tighten the lids. Let the jars cool (this helps preserve the fruit).

Makes 4 1/4 cups or 2 pints

rumtopf

see variations page 166

This Danish and German Christmas dessert is traditionally made in a pot set in a cool and dark place in spring. Different kinds of fruit are added to it in layers over the months as they come in season, and it's eaten in the depths of winter.

1/4 cup nectarine (pitted)
5 tbsp. white rum (50 percent proof)
1/2 cup granulated fructose
1/4 cup black currants

1/4 cup raspberries (hulled)
1/4 cup strawberries (hulled)
1/4 cup blackberries (hulled)
1/4 cup peaches (pitted)

Take a large, sterilized jar and put 2 1/2 tablespoons rum at the bottom, along with a layer of nectarines. Top with 4 teaspoons fructose. Then place a layer of blackcurrants in the jar and top with 4 teaspoons fructose. Next, add a layer of raspberries and 4 teaspoons of fructose; a layer of strawberries topped with 4 teaspoons of fructose; then a layer of blackberries topped with 4 teaspoons of fructose. Finally, add the peaches; top with 4 teaspoons of fructose, and 2 1/2 tablespoons rum. If there is still space in the jar, add extra fruit, sugar, and rum until the jar is full. Store in a cool dark place until Christmas.

If fruit rises, add additional layers of fruit, sugar and rum; the fruit should always be submerged to prevent mold from growing. Ideally, the first layer should be added in June with the first fruits of the summer and additional layers added every 2–3 weeks. The final layer should be added by the end of September. Set aside to infuse for 4 months and enjoy at Christmas.

Makes 1 tall jar (1 pint jar)

spiced whole clementines

see variations page 167

I love clementines, but their season just isn't long enough! Before they get tough and dry, can them with this recipe so you can enjoy them all year round.

10 clementines
1 cup light brown muscovado sugar
1 cinnamon stick
5 cloves

5 allspice berries
1 1/2 cups water
1 1/2 cups brandy
juice of 1 lemon

Use a sharp knife to cut a small cross at the top and base of each clementine. This will help with peeling. Put them in a bowl and cover with boiling water. Leave for a few minutes. Remove a clementine and try to peel it. If it peels easily, peel the other clementines. Carefully scrape away the pith because it will make the preserve bitter.

Add the sugar, cinnamon stick, cloves, all spice berries and water to a large pan. Heat gently until the sugar has dissolved. Increase the heat and bring to a boil. Simmer until the mixture turns syrupy. Add the peeled clementines and brandy to the pan and cook for another 15–20 minutes. Remove from the heat and add the lemon juice.

Put the fruit into the jar and pour the brandy syrup over it. Seal and store in the refrigerator. Consume within 4 weeks.

Makes 4 1/4 cups

black currants in gin syrup

see variations page 168

These purple goodies are worth their weight in gold. A great store cupboard standby for an impromptu dessert with lots of cream.

1/2 cup superfine or baker's sugar
1/2 cup gin
1/2 cup water

1 lb 2 oz black currants
1 teaspoon fresh mint

Make the gin syrup – put the sugar, gin and water in a pan and bring to a boil until the sugar dissolves. Reduce the liquid until a syrup forms.

The jar should be warm and sterilized. Place the washed black currants into the jar (make sure that they are as snug as a bug). Pour the gin syrup and mint over the black currants. Put the lid on, turning only half way – this will help the steam escape.

Place the jar in a pan and cover it up to the shoulder with warm water. Gently heat the water to a simmer and simmer for 25 minutes. Remove the hot jar carefully and tighten the lid. Let cool (this helps to preserve the fruit).

Makes 1 medium-sized jar

brandied strawberries & peaches

see variations page 169

Bottled summer! These deliciously infused vanilla peaches & strawberries are the perfect topping for strawberry ice cream and great stacks of pancakes.

3 large peaches
4 oz strawberries, hulled
3/4 cup sugar
1 vanilla pod

3 cloves
2 1/2 cups eau de vie (clear, colorless fruit brandy)

Using a sharp knife, cut a small cross at the base of each peach. This will help with peeling the peach. Put the peaches in a bowl and cover with boiling water. Let the peaches sit for a few minutes. Remove a peach and try to peel it. If the skin comes off easily, peel the other peaches. If not, put the peach back in the hot water and try again in a few minutes.

Once all the skins are removed, cut the peaches in halves and then into quarters. Discard the pits. Arrange the peaches and whole strawberries in layers in the jar, alternating with layers of the sugar. Place the vanilla pod down one side of the jar and the cloves down the other side of the jar.

Pour the eau de vie over the fruit, making sure that the fruit is completely covered. Seal and then shake the jar gently to help dissolve the sugar. Store the jar in a dark place for a couple of months. Shake the jar gently once a week. Enjoy after 2 months.

Makes 1 quart Kilner jar

drunken raspberries

see base recipe page 157

drunken blackberries
Replace the raspberries with blackberries; replace the vodka with cassis (black currant liqueur).

drunken blues
Replace the raspberries with blueberries. Replace the vodka with orange liqueur and add the zest of 1 orange when cooking the blueberries.

strawberry heaven
Replace the raspberries with strawberries; replace the vodka with strawberry flavored whiskey or sloe gin. Add the zest of 1 lime and the juice.

drunken peaches
Replace the raspberries with halved peaches; omit the rose water and replace it with 1 cinnamon stick. Cook with the skinned halved peaches.

non-alcoholic preserved raspberries
If you want to serve this to your kids, remove the vodka and add raspberry juice instead.

variations

rumtopf

see base recipe page 159

clippy's gin rumtopf
Replace the rum with gin.

non-alcoholic rumtopf
Replace the alcohol with orange juice. Without the addition of alcohol, this preserve will need to go straight in the refrigerator. Eat within 1 week of making.

traditional rumtopf
Replace the fruit sugar with light brown sugar; add 1 clove to each layer, along with the sugar and alcohol.

your own mix rumtopf
Use any fruits you like and follow the recipe. Hard fruits don't really work very well.

spiced whole clementines

see base recipe page 161

clementines, vanilla & orange liqueur
Replace the brandy with an orange liqueur; replace all the spices with
2 vanilla pods.

tangerine & kumquat
Substitute tangerines for the clementines and add 10 kumquats and
continue with the recipe.

pears with cinnamon, cloves and brandy
Replace the clementines with pears (small whole pears are best); follow
the recipe.

pears in mulled wine
Replace the brandy with red wine; add a teaspoon of allspice berries.
Proceed as main recipe.

spiced peaches
Replace the clementines with peaches; replace the brandy with dark rum.

variations

black currants in gin syrup

see base recipe page 162

blueberries in a gin syrup
Replace black currants with blueberries; follow the recipe.

cherries submerged in kirsch
Replace the black currants with cherries; replace the gin with Kirsch (cherry brandy). Omit the mint.

fruit salad
Pick your favorite fruits and omit the mint; replace the mint with a split vanilla pod.

chardonnay pears
Omit the black currants, mint, and gin. Replace with chardonnay and small pears; follow the recipe. Add 1 cinnamon stick and 10 whole cloves.

honeyed pears
Same recipe as above; replace half the sugar with honey.

brandied strawberries and peaches

see base recipe page 164

brandied nectarines & raspberries
Replace the peaches with nectarines; replace the strawberries with raspberries.

honeyed brandied fruits
Replace the sugar with a flavored honey and follow the recipe.

lavender infused strawberries & peaches
Omit the cloves and vanilla. Add 1 teaspoon lavender and top with the eau de vie.

sugar syrup fruits
Remove the alcohol. Make a sugar syrup solution of half water and half sugar. Make enough to cover the fruits and then gently pasteurize them. Follow the Drunken Raspberries recipe (on page 157).

cordials

My all-time favourite homemade cordial is traditional lemonade topped off with sparkling water, but I've got a soft spot for the raspberry, rose & vanilla cordial too! Essentially these preserves are made using fruit and sugar either are heated and bottled immediately, or set aside to macerate over a few days. All of the cordials in this chapter should be diluted with still or sparkling water in a ratio of 1 part cordial to 4 parts water.

st clements cordial

see variations page 182

The simple combination of oranges and lemons topped off with sparkling water is a match made in heaven.

1 litre (1¾ pints) water
1kg (2 lbs 3 oz) light muscovado sugar

10 lemons
11 oranges

Heat the water and sugar together until dissolved. Zest 5 lemons and 5 oranges (be careful not to get the pith, because this will make the cordial bitter). Squeeze the juice from the oranges and lemons and add it to the sugar solution along with the fruit zest.

Bring to the boil and pour it into warm sterilized bottles with a screw top. Store in a cool, dark place for a couple of days before opening.

Makes approximately 1.5 litres (2¾ pints)

four-berry cordial

see variations page 183

This fruity concoction is so much fun to make. Make sure you wear rubber gloves; otherwise, your hands will be stained a lovely purple hue! I've replaced the sugar with fructose for those watching the calories.

300g (10½ oz) blackcurrants
200g (7 oz) redcurrants
200g (7 oz) blackberries
200g (7 oz) raspberries

200ml (7 fl. oz) lemon juice (freshly squeezed)
300g (10½ oz) fructose
1 litre (1¾ pints) water

Clean and rinse the fruit and remove the stalks and tufts from the currants. Add them to a deep bowl along with the berries. Pour the freshly squeezed lemon juice over the berries and stir. In a pan, heat the sugar and water together until the sugar has dissolved. Add the sugar mixture to the fruit mixture. Set aside for a couple of hours while the fruit and liquid work their magic.

Once the mixture has cooled, cover with a clean towel and let stand in a cool, dark place for at least 24 hours. To extract the berry cordial, place the contents in a sieve set over a bowl (don't squeeze the mixture or you'll get a cloudy cordial). Decant the cordial into clean, sterilized bottles with secure lids.

Makes approximately 1.2 litres (2 pints)

strawberry & mint cordial

see variations page 184

The combination of juicy red strawberries and a hint of mint make this a winner! Serve with ice and enjoy the fruits of your labor. In other cordials, the fruit is steeped for 24 hours, but strawberries get too mushy with steeping, so they're best cooked.

1kg (2 lbs 3 oz) strawberries (hulled)
500g (1 lb 2 oz) sugar

5 tbsp. freshly chopped mint
1 litre (1¾ pints) water

Place all the ingredients into a deep pan and bring it to a boil. Simmer for 20 minutes, until all the juice has run from the strawberries. Let cool.

To extract the juice, place the contents in a sieve set over a bowl (don't squeeze the mixture or you'll get a cloudy cordial). Decant into clean, sterilized bottles with secure lids. Store in the refrigerator and use within 2 weeks.

Makes approximately 1.2 litres (2 pints)

raspberry, rose & vanilla cordial

see variations page 185

I love the beautiful aroma of vanilla and rose mixed together. I once had the pleasure of enjoying this truly intoxicating cordial at a very posh hotel for breakfast, and this is my version.

1kg (2 lbs 3 oz) raspberries (hulled)
5 tbsp. lemon juice
500g (1 lb 2 oz) sugar

2 vanilla pods
1 litre (1¾ pints) water
5 tbsp. rose syrup

Rinse the raspberries, and place them in a large bowl. Pour the freshly squeezed lemon juice over the berries and stir.

In a pan, heat the sugar, split vanilla pods, and water together until the sugar has dissolved, then add this to the raspberries. Let stand for a good couple of hours while the fruit marinates with the vanilla mixture.

Once the mixture is cool, add the rose syrup and cover with a clean towel. Set aside in a cool, dark place for at least 24 hours.

To extract the raspberry juice, place the contents in a sieve set over a bowl (don't squeeze the mixture or you'll get a cloudy cordial). Decant into clean, sterilized bottles with secure lids.

Makes approximately 1 litre (1¾ pints)

ginger cordial

see variations page 186

I often serve this cordial hot in the winter for a traditional hot toddy, along with lemon slices and a glug of whiskey and honey.

1 large piece ginger (peeled and sliced)
1 lemon (peel & juice only)
1 tsp. cream of tartar

200g (7 oz light brown muscovado sugar
2.5 litres (4½ pints) boiling water

Place the ginger, lemons, lemon juice, cream of tartar, and sugar in a deep bowl. Cover with the boiling water and stir to dissolve the sugar. Set aside in a cool, dark place for 3–4 days.

To extract the ginger juice, place the contents in a sieve set over a bowl (don't squeeze the mixture or you'll get a cloudy cordial). Decant into clean, sterilized bottles with secure lids. Store in the refrigerator and use within 2 weeks. Top with sparkling water for a refreshing drink.

Makes approximately 1 litre (1¾ pints)

traditional lemonade

see variations page 187

Sweet, juicy, and tart all at the same time; it's a taste explosion. Serve immediately over ice or topped with cool sparkling water.

6 large lemons
200g (7 oz) sugar
1.4 litres (2½ pints) boiling water

Scrub the lemons, and then peel (be careful that you only peel the skin and not the pith, because the pith will make the lemonade bitter) and juice the lemons. In a deep bowl, add the sugar, lemon peelings, and juice. Pour the boiling water over the lemons, stir to dissolve the sugar, and cover. Set aside in a cool, dark place for 24 hours.

To extract the lemon juice, place the contents in a sieve set over a bowl (don't squeeze the mixture or you'll get a cloudy cordial). Decant into clean, sterilized bottles with secure lids. Store in the refrigerator and use within 2 weeks.

Makes approximately 1.5 litres (2¾ pints)

variations

st clements cordial

see base recipe page 171

lemon & lime cordial
Halve the number of lemons and replace them with limes.

vanilla st clements cordial
Add the seeds from 1 vanilla pod when simmering the cordial.

elderflower st clements
Add several elderflower heads when simmering the cordial; remove them when you decant the cordial.

honeyed st clements
When simmering the cordial, add 5 tablespoons runny honey.

saffron-infused st clements
Add a big pinch of saffron when simmering the fruit.

variations

four-berry cordial

see base recipe page 173

cinnamon four-berry cordial
Add a cinnamon stick and a split vanilla pod when adding the sugar/water solution to the fruit; discard when decanting.

four-berry cordial
Replace the blackberries with strawberries.

spiced four-berry cordial
Bruise 10 cardamom pods and place them in a muslin bag; infuse with the fruit. Discard the muslin bag when decanting.

honeyed four-berry cordial
Add 10 tablespoons of runny honey to the fruity mix and halve the amount of sugar.

cherryberry cordial
Replace the blackberries with cherries. Add 1 tablespoon almond extract just before decanting.

strawberry & mint cordial

see base recipe page 174

blueberry bay cordial
Replace the strawberries with blueberries. Replace the mint with 6 fresh bay leaves. Make sure the blueberries are soft before extracting the juice.

blueberry & lemon verbena
Replace the strawberries with blueberries; add a few sprigs of lemon verbena or lemon balm when cooking the blueberries.

strawberry, mint & raspberry cordial
Halve the amount of strawberries and replace with raspberries; continue with the recipe.

lemon strawberry delight
Omit the mint. Replace half the strawberries with lemons (zest and juice), and then follow the recipe.

strawberry & vanilla cordial
Add the seeds from 2 vanilla pods when cooking the strawberries; omit the mint.

raspberry, rose & vanilla cordial

see base recipe page 177

blackberry cordial
Replace the raspberries with blackberries; replace the rose syrup with half a nutmeg. Add nutmeg along with the blackberries.

orange & raspberry cordial
Replace half the raspberries with the oranges (zest and juice them); add to the raspberries and continue with the recipe. Omit the lemon juice.

raspberry lime cordial
Add the zest and juice of 2 limes to the raspberries. Omit the lemon juice.

spiced raspberry blue cordial
Replace half the raspberries with blueberries and add ½ teaspoon ground cinnamon, ¼ teaspoon nutmeg, ¼ teaspoon ground cloves. Add these along with fruit.

variations

ginger cordial

see base recipe page 178

ginger & honey cordial
Add 6 tablespoons honey with the sugar.

ginger & lemon cordial
Add another 2 lemons and follow the recipe. Add another 100g (3½ oz) sugar.

ginger & marmalade cordial
Use 2 Seville oranges instead of the lemon. Replace the light brown sugar with granulated sugar. The marmalade flavour comes from the Seville oranges.

pink grapefruit & ginger cordial
Replace the lemon with 1 large grapefruit and continue with the recipe.

gingered apple cordial
Slice 3 peeled and cored apples and add along with the remaining ingredients.

traditional lemonade

see base recipe page 181

limeade
Replace 3 lemons with 3 limes, and follow the recipe.

minted lemonade
Add 12 sprigs of mint along with the lemons, and then follow the recipe.

orangeade
Replace the lemons with oranges, and follow the recipe.

cherryade
Replace the lemons with 450g (1 lb) cherries (pitted); add the zest from 1 lime. Add the lime zest along with the hot water.

relishes

Not just for your cheese board: add a dollop to your favourite casserole or spread liberally on a grilled cheese sandwich! They are a mixture of spices, fruit and/or vegetables, vinegars, and herbs similar to chutney but with less cooking time. Relishes are generally diced into smaller pieces, compared to chutney, with less vinegar and a bit more sugar.

sticky onion relish

see variations page 201

Delicious with all kinds of barbecued meats, fish, and portobello mushrooms with melted blue cheese and a sprinkling of toasted walnuts.

3 tbsp. sunflower oil
700g (1 lb 8 oz) white onions, finely sliced
160g (5½ oz) natural molasses sugar
55g (2 oz) light muscovado sugar

5½ tbsp. cider vinegar
2 tbsp. dry cider
pinch flaked salt
pinch freshly ground pepper

Add the oil to a pan on a medium heat, then add the onions; sweat them for approximately 5 minutes and turn down the heat. Cook gently for another 25 minutes, until they start to change colour and become translucent. The mixture should start to get thick and juicy (stir frequently to prevent the relish from burning – especially in the last 15 minutes).

Once your first cook has finished, add the sugars, and stir until the sugars are dissolved. Continue to cook for another 10 minutes (watch your pan carefully; you don't want to burn the relish). The relish should be quite thick and glossy.

Then add the cider vinegar, cider, salt, and pepper and cook rapidly for another 10–15 minutes. You will know when it's ready because the onions will be soft and have a slight bite to them. The relish should be thick and sticky. Use within 12 months.

Makes 450g (1 lb)

apple, beetroot & lemon relish

see variations page 202

It's well worth roasting the beetroot 24 hours before using them in this robust and tangy relish. Serve with a watercress and goat's cheese salad.

500g (1 lb 2 oz) cooking apples (peeled & cored) chopped
500g (1 lb 2 oz) beetroot, peeled & diced
2 tbsp. vegetable oil
1 lemon (zest only)
2 tbsp. grated ginger
1 tbsp. chopped garlic

1 tbsp. lemon juice
1 tsp. ground allspice
100g (3½ oz) red onions sliced and diced (once peeled)
200ml (7 fl. oz) red wine vinegar
200g (7 oz) light brown muscovado sugar

Roast the beetroot for approximately 1 hour with the oil, and set aside. Add all the ingredients to your pan (except for the sugar, roasted beetroot and vinegar), combine the ingredients and cook on a medium heat for about 10 minutes. Add the vinegar and cook for another 10 minutes.

The mixture should start to get thick and juicy (stir frequently to prevent the chutney burning — especially in the first 5 minutes). Once your first cook has finished, add the sugar and beetroot. Stir until the sugar is dissolved. Crank up the heat and cook for another 15–20 minutes (watch your pan carefully; it should only simmer). The relish should be quite thick. You may need to add a little water to the last cook if your mixture is quite dry.

Always taste your chutney before potting. If needed, add additional spices to your taste. Use within 12 months.

Makes 1.1kg (2 lbs 4 oz)

balsamic & red onion relish

see variations page 203

For you adventurous types, try adding this relish as a topping for goat's cheese & rocket pizza. It's also a match made in heaven with veggie or pork sausages and hot dogs.

700g (1 lb 8 oz) red onions, sliced
3 tbsp. sunflower oil
1 bay leaf
1 tbsp. freshly chopped rosemary
200g (7 oz) sugar

2 tbsp. white balsamic vinegar
5½ tbsp. white wine vinegar
pinch flaked salt
pinch freshly ground pepper

Add the oil to a pan on a medium heat, and then add the onions. Sweat them for approximately 5 minutes; turn down the heat. Add the bay leaf and rosemary and cook gently for a further 25 minutes, until the onions start to change colour and become translucent. The mixture should start to get thick and juicy (stir frequently to prevent the relish burning — especially in the last 15 minutes).

Once your 1st cook has finished, add the sugar, and stir until the sugar is dissolved. Continue to cook for another 10 minutes (watch your pan closely; you don't want to burn the relish). The relish should be quite thick and glossy.

Then add the vinegars, salt, and pepper and cook rapidly for another 10–15 minutes. You will know when it's ready because the onions will be soft and have a slight bite to them, and the relish should be thick and sticky. Spoon the relish into pre-sterilized jars and seal. Set aside for a week or so for the flavours to harmonize, and use within 12 months.

Makes 450g (1 lb)

sweet corn & chili relish

see variations page 204

This time-honoured American relish is superb with hot dogs, chicken wings, or a big bowl of beef chili and tacos.

1 large red bell pepper (roasted)
5 large ears of corn (with husks and silk removed)
1/4 white cabbage (roughly chopped)
1 medium white onion (skinned and halved)
2 tsp. ground turmeric

1 tsp. mustard powder
2 tbsp. flour
1/2 medium red chili (deseeded & diced)
150g (51/2 oz) sugar
500ml (16 fl. oz) cider vinegar
2 tbsp. maple syrup

Place the pepper in the oven for about 20–30 minutes and roast until blackened on all sides. Remove the pepper and seal in a paper bag; this makes it easier to peel and deseed. Set it aside for 10 minutes. Then skin, seed, and dice. Cook the ears of corn in boiling water for about 3–5 minutes; drain. Using a sharp knife, cut the corn away from the cobs (be careful, because this is quite tricky). If you have a food processor, coarsely mince the cabbage and halved onions. Combine the corn, diced peppers, cabbage, and onions in a bowl.

In a separate bowl, blend the turmeric, mustard powder, flour, and chili. Add a slug of vinegar to create a paste and then gradually add the remaining vinegar. Dissolve the sugar, and maple syrup over a low heat; once dissolved, bring to a simmering boil. At this point, add the prepared vegetables and simmer for 30 minutes. Let cool for 5 minutes and then spoon into clean, sterilized jars and seal.

Makes 2.1kg (4 lbs 10 oz)

spiced gooseberry relish

see variations page 205

I made this preserve in the summer and it kept beautifully as a winter relish. Add to leftover ham, turkey, and stuffing for a delicious sandwich.

650g (1 lb 6 oz) gooseberries
100g (3½ oz) red onions
4½ tbsp. white wine vinegar
1 tsp. cinnamon

2 teaspoons ground ginger
2 teaspoons apple pie spice
400g (14 oz) light brown sugar
small handful sultanas

Add all the ingredients to your pan except the sugar. Stir the ingredients and cook on a medium heat for about 20 minutes. Make sure that the gooseberry skins are soft before adding the sugar. The mixture should start to get thick and juicy (stir frequently to prevent the relish burning – especially in the first 5 minutes).

Once your first cook has finished, add the sugar and stir until the sugar is dissolved. Turn up the heat to a simmering boil and simmer for another 10–15 minutes (watch your pan carefully; it should only simmer).

Always taste your relish before potting. You will know if the relish is ready by trying a sultana; it should be plump and have a slight taste of vinegar but not sharp. Once ready, spoon into sterilized jars and seal. Use within 12 months.

Makes 600g (1 lb 5 oz)

spiced plumberry relish

see variations page 206

This is truly delicious; a real dinner-time treat served with pan-fried salmon and wilted greens. Create your own luxury cheeseboard with cured hams and chunks of fresh baked bread.

200g (7 oz) cooking apples (weight once peeled, cored and chopped)
200g (7 oz) plums (weight once halved and pitted)
1 small red onion (peeled and diced)
2 teaspoons freshly grated ginger
½ tsp. crushed dried chili flakes

1 tsp. fresh diced garlic
1 tsp. lemon juice
3 tbsp. water
150g (5½ oz) blackberries (hulled)
170g (6 oz) granulated fructose
5 tbsp. red wine vinegar

Put the chopped apples, plum halves, red onions, spices, lemon juice, and water into a preserving pan with the lid on. Bring to a gentle boil and then simmer until the plums and apples have broken down and are soft and pulpy, approximately 10–15 minutes. Add the blackberries and cook the little beauties until they soften, approximately 5–10 minutes.

Add the fructose and vinegar, stirring until dissolved. Do not replace the lid because you want to reduce the mixture to a jam consistency.

Bring to a simmering boil; your relish should be ready in 4–6 minutes. You can test the relish by tasting to make sure it is not too vinegary; it should have a sweet but sour flavour. Pour into sterilized jars. Store in a cool place and use within 12 months.

Makes 600g (1 lb 5 oz)

hot and sunny tomato relish

see variations page 207

This condiment is perfect with fried foods, such as calamari, grilled cheese, or falafel.

600g (1 lb 5 oz) large tomatoes (skinned)
2 large shallots, roasted (once peeled)
3 roasted garlic cloves (see method below)
1 pinch saffron

100ml (3½ fl. oz) red wine vinegar
½ medium-sized fresh red chili (sliced)
100g (3½ oz) caster sugar
7 tbsp. honey

First score the ends of the tomatoes and place them in a bowl. Pour hot water over them until covered. Set aside for 20 minutes; peel the tomatoes. Let cool.

Place the shallots and garlic in a preheated 350°F oven for approximately 20–30 minutes, until soft but not burnt. Remove and let cool.

Place the tomatoes, roasted chopped onions, garlic, saffron, vinegar, chili, and cook for 10–15 minutes, until the tomatoes have lost their tart bite and are starting to break down. Then add the sugar and honey and cook for another 5–10 minutes.

Spoon into cool, sterilized jars and seal. Set aside for a couple of weeks to let the flavours harmonize. Once opened, store in the refrigerator and eat within 6 weeks.

Makes 600g (1 lb 5 oz)

sticky onion relish

see base recipe page 189

sticky shallot relish
Replace the white onions with shallots; replace the cider with Guinness.

sticky red onion
Replace the white onions with red onions; replace the cider vinegar with red wine vinegar. Omit the cider.

apple & sticky onion relish
Replace half the onions with cooking apples (peeled, cored and chopped); add the apples in the last 20 minutes of the first cooking stage.

spanish sticky onion relish
Add ¼ teaspoon smoked paprika, and ½ teaspoon freshly chopped garlic; replace the vinegar with sherry wine vinegar. Omit the cider and spices.

spiced sticky onion relish
Replace the onions with shallots; add 1 teaspoon apple pie spice when cooking the onions. Replace the sugar with fructose.

variations

apple, roasted beetroot & lemon relish

see base recipe page 191

pears, beetroot & lemon relish
Replace the cooking apples with pears; substitute the ground allspice for 1 teaspoon freshly chopped red chili.

pears, beetroot & ginger
Replace the apples with pears; add 2 extra tablespoons ginger for a kicking relish.

roasted fruits & beetroot relish
Replace half the apples with pears (peel, core and chop); add the fruit, half the vinegar, and half the sugar in the last 30 minutes when roasting the beetroot. Then follow the recipe.

moroccan relish
Add ½ teaspoon ground cumin, 2 tablespoons freshly grated horseradish, and ¼ teaspoon ground coriander.

beetroot, chili & balsamic relish
Don't roast the beetroot, but grate them coarsely. Add them to the apples and remaining ingredients, along with ½ teaspoon dried chili flakes. Replace the red wine vinegar with balsamic vinegar.

balsamic & red onion relish

see base recipe page 192

sweet summer night relish
Add the zest from 1 orange and 1 lemon at the beginning of cooking.

onion marmalade
Add 250ml (9 fl. oz) red wine vinegar and half the amount of sugar; replace the rosemary with fresh bay leaves.

caramelized red onion relish
Replace the oil with butter; replace the rosemary with 1 red chili (sliced), and replace the granulated sugar with dark brown sugar.

sweet thyme & red onion relish
Replace the rosemary with thyme. Replace the vinegars with red wine vinegar. Replace the white sugar with light brown sugar.

fruity red onion relish
Replace half the onions with redcurrants, and follow the recipe.

variations

sweet corn & chili relish

see base recipe page 194

sweet corn & coriander relish
Add a handful of freshly chopped coriander leaves just before potting.

sweet & spicy sweet corn relish
Omit the cabbage and replace it with 3 sticks of celery (diced); add ½ teaspoon celery seeds. Omit the maple syrup and replace it with light brown sugar.

sweet corn burger relish
Omit the maple syrup and add the zest and juice from 1 lime; replace the sugar with honey.

sweet corn & pepper relish
Replace the cabbage with 1 red pepper (chopped) and 1 chargrilled green pepper.

hot sweet corn chili relish
Add 1 tablespoon dried chili flakes.

spiced gooseberry relish

see base recipe page 197

spiced rhubarb relish
Replace the gooseberries with rhubarb; use freshly grated ginger instead of ground ginger.

fruity relish
Replace the gooseberries with equal amounts of cranberries, raspberries, and the zest and juice from 3 oranges.

caribbean relish
Replace the gooseberries with equal amounts of mango and pineapple (diced). Add the zest and juice from 1 lime.

peachy pear relish
Replace the gooseberries with equal amounts of peaches (pitted, peeled, and chopped) pears (peeled, cored, and chopped). Replace the vinegar with red wine vinegar. Omit the dried fruit.

gooseberry lemon relish
Omit the dried fruit and replace it with the zest from 2 lemons. Replace the red onion with shallots; replace the spices with ½ teaspoon freshly chopped garlic, ½ teaspoon freshly grated ginger, and 1 teaspoon freshly chopped red chili.

variations

spiced plumberry relish

see base recipe page 198

plumberry pear relish
Replace the cooking apples with pears; replace the onions with shallots; replace the sugar with light brown sugar. Add the zest of 1 orange with the sugar.

apple plum relish
Omit the blackberries and replace them with extra cooking apples. Replace the fruit sugar with light brown sugar; replace the spices with 1 teaspoon of apple pie spice.

autumnal plumberry relish
Replace half the apples with pears and roast the plums, apples and pears. Sprinkle with half the vinegar and sugar; cook in the oven until the juice turns into a syrup and the fruit is soft to the touch. Transfer to a pan and add the spices, remaining sugar, and vinegar; proceed as main recipe.

spiced plumberry relish
Omit the spices and replace them with pickling spices in a muslin bag (½ teaspoon mustard seeds, 1 teaspoon peppercorns, ½ teaspoon cloves, ½ teaspoon juniper berries, ½ teaspoon mace blade, and ½ teaspoon small dried ginger).

hot and sunny tomato relish

see base recipe page 200

cherry tomato relish
replace vine tomatoes with yellow and red cherry tomatoes.

roasted hot cherry tomato relish
Roast the tomatoes, along with the garlic, shallots, and ½ teaspoon chopped
fresh thyme.

indian summer tomato relish
Add ½ teaspoon ground cumin, ground coriander, and 1 teaspoon fresh
thyme. Omit the chili.

allotment relish
Replace half the tomatoes with cooking apples (peeled, cored, chopped);
don't roast the garlic or onions but peel and chop them. Replace the honey
with light brown sugar. Replace the chili with 1 teaspoon mustard seeds.

smokin' hot & sunny tomato relish
Add ½ teaspoon smoked paprika and replace the salt with smoked salt; add
1 chargrilled red pepper (skinned and sliced).

pickles

There are two types of pickles — sweet and clear. Sweet pickles, like my Mostarda di Frutta, are often flavoured with a spiced sweet vinegar syrup, fruits, vegetables, and sugar. In clear pickles, such as pickling pickled pears or pickled shallots, the fruit or vegetables are generally left whole, sometimes brined overnight or poached and then flavoured with vinegar, spices, wine, honey, and sugar.

spiced pears

see variations page 220

I serve pickled pears with a smorgasbord of cheeses, cured meats, pâtés, and fresh baked bread. There are several varieties to choose from, but I love the blush pears for this recipe, juicy and sweet.

200ml (7 fl. oz) white wine vinegar
200g (7 oz) sugar
1 cinnamon stick

10 cloves
1 tsp. allspice berries
3 small pears

Add the white wine vinegar, sugar, cinnamon, cloves, and allspice berries to a pan. Gently simmer until the sugar has dissolved; then bring the mixture to a boil. Put the lid on the pan and turn down the heat to a gentle simmer.

Peel the pears (try to leave them whole with the stalks attached). Add the pears to the hot spiced vinegar; gently simmer with the lid on until they are tender, approximately 10 minutes. Put the spiced pears in the sterilized jars.

Meanwhile, bring the spiced vinegar slowly to the boil and cook for another minute. Pour the spiced vinegar carefully over the pears (if you want, add the cinnamon stick to the pears). Seal and store for at least 4 weeks.

Makes 1 medium-sized jar

pickled shallots

see variations page 221

This recipe is for quite crunchy pickled shallots, which are the perfect foil to a sharp Cheddar cheese.

1kg (2 lbs 4 oz) shallots, peeled, and topped
    and tailed)
250g (9 oz) flaked salt
2 litres (4½ pints) water
700ml (1¼ pints) white wine vinegar
180g (6 oz) light muscovado sugar

1 tbsp. red, green, black peppercorns
1 tbsp. juniper berries
1 tbsp. allspice berries
2 bay leaves
1 cinnamon stick

First, brine the shallots for at least 24 hours: top and tail the shallots; add the salt and the water to a pan and bring to a boil. Remove from the heat, pour the liquid into a deep bowl, and place the shallots in the brine overnight (ideally, 24 hours).

The next day, put the vinegar, sugar, and spices into a saucepan and bring to a boil. Turn off the heat and let cool for 10–15 minutes. (If you want softer shallots, don't let cool; pour the hot vinegar over the shallots.)

Drain the shallots and rinse them in very cold water. Carefully pack into the cool, sterilized jars. Pour the infused vinegar and spices over the shallots. Cover the jars and leave in a cool, dark place for 3–4 weeks before eating.

Makes 1.2kg (2 lbs 10 oz)

classic piccalilli

see variations page 222

This sweet vegetable pickle hails from India, and the combination of really fresh vegetables and spices makes this a truly delightful preserve.

1 small head cauliflower, broken into florets
3 or 4 small pickling onions
1kg (2 lbs 4 oz) mixed vegetables
3½ tbsp. flaked salt
1 tbsp. turmeric

2 tbsp. English mustard powder
2 tbsp. plain flour
1 tsp. ground ginger
800ml (1⅓ pints) cider vinegar
300g (10½ oz) sugar

Leave the pickling onions whole and cut the remaining vegetables into bite-sized pieces. It's important that they are all similar in size, so there's consistency in the final pickle. Place all the vegetables in a large bowl and sprinkle with the flaked salt. Mix the ingredients and cover and leave in a cool, dark place for 24 hours. Then rinse the vegetables several times in cold, fresh water and set aside.

In a large pan, mix the turmeric, English mustard powder, flour, and ground ginger with a slug of vinegar to create a paste and then gradually add the remaining vinegar, stirring all the time. Add the sugar and dissolve the sugar over a low heat. Once the sugar is dissolved, bring to simmering boil; keep stirring until all the visible lumps have disappeared (approximately 5 minutes). Remove the pan from the heat and add the vegetables to the thickened sauce. Stir well until the vegetables are fully coated. Spoon into the cooled, sterilized jars. Allow to mature for at least 6 weeks.

Makes 2kg (4 lbs 8 oz)

green bean pickle

see variations page 223

These hot, nutty little beans are so versatile; add to tomato sauce for pasta, chop finely for a tartar sauce for homemade fish & chips or use as a topping for pizza!

1 tbsp. flaked salt
300ml (½ pint) cold water
125g (4½ oz) fresh green beans, topped and
    tailed

170ml (6 fl. oz) cider vinegar
3 cloves garlic, minced
1 tsp. dried chili flakes
1 tsp. dill seeds

First, brine the beans for at least 24 hours: add the salt and the water to a pan and bring to a boil. Remove from the heat, pour the liquid into a deep bowl, and place the beans in the brine overnight (ideally, 24 hours).

The following day, discard the brine, and wash and dry the beans really well. Gently simmer the vinegar, garlic, and spices approximately 5 minutes. Add the beans to the jar leaving a 1-mm (¹/₁₆-in.) gap at the top of the jar. Cover with the spiced vinegar.

Leave in a cool, dry dark place for about 2 weeks before eating.

Makes 1 medium-sized jar

best-ever spiced pickled eggs

see variations page 224

My fiancé's mother, Irene, makes the best-ever pickled eggs. Every Christmas these little beauties adorn the buffet table. It's really important to use really good spiced vinegar to infuse the oval gems.

12 extra-large organic eggs
350ml (12 fl. oz) cider vinegar
350ml (12 fl. oz) water
1 cinnamon stick
½ tsp. mustard seeds
1 tsp. peppercorns
½ tsp. cloves

½ tsp. juniper berries
½ tsp. mace
½ tsp. dill seeds
small piece dried ginger
1 clove garlic, crushed
1 bay leaf

Place the eggs in a saucepan and cover with cold water. Bring the water to a boil and immediately remove from the heat. Cover and let the eggs stand in the hot water for 10 to 12 minutes. Remove the eggs from the hot water; cool and peel.

In a medium saucepan over medium heat, mix together the vinegar, water, and all pickling spices, apart from the crushed garlic and bay leaf. Bring to a boil and then add the garlic and bay leaf. Remove from the heat.

Transfer the eggs to sterilized containers. Strain the vinegar and keep the spices. Fill the containers with the hot spiced vinegar; then spread the seeds equally among the jars. Seal and shake to disperse the spices. Refrigerate for 2 weeks before serving.

Makes 2 medium-sized jars

mostarda di frutta

see variations page 225

Mostarda di Frutta is an Italian delicacy and is often paired with cured meats, such as salami, and cheeses. The name mostarda suggests that it's a mustard, but it's actually a fruit preserve spiced with mustard oil. It can be difficult to find mustard oil, so I suggest using mustard seeds and powder to pep up the flavour.

150g (5½ oz) dried figs
150g (5½ oz) unsulfured dried apricots
100g (3½ oz) dried prunes
100g (3½ oz) glacé cherries
2 large oranges, juiced and finely zested

300ml (10 fl. oz) water
2 tbsp. English mustard powder
3 tbsp. yellow mustard seeds
120ml (4 fl. oz) white wine vinegar
120ml (4 fl. oz) orange blossom honey

When selecting your dried fruit, choose ones that look perfect, because they are kept whole throughout the process. Place the dried and glacé fruits into a deep bowl and pour the freshly squeezed orange juice, orange zest, and water over them. Stir to combine. Cover and leave overnight to marinate.

The following day, blend the mustard powder and seeds with a little of the vinegar; gradually add the remaining vinegar until it is combined. Place the orange soaked fruit into a pan and heat gently until simmering; the smell is intoxicating. Add the honey and stir to combine. Add the blended mustard powder and seeds to the fruity mix and stir well, until there are no visible lumps. Simmer for approximately 15–20 minutes, stirring occasionally; the mixture will become thick and glossy. Remove from the heat and spoon into sterilized jars. Seal and store for 3–4 weeks. This preserve will keep for up to 12 months unopened.

Makes 1kg (2 lbs 4 oz)

variations

spiced pears

see base recipe page 209

pickled peaches
Replace the pears with peaches. You'll need to remove the skins, so score them at each end and place them in boiling hot water; after 2–3 minutes, remove and skin them. Then follow the recipe.

peaches & star anise
Replace the pears with peaches and omit the allspice berries and cloves; replace with 3 star anise.

mulled cider pears
Replace half the vinegar with cider and continue cooking.

pickled lemons
Omit the sugar and replace it with salt; omit the pears and replace them with 10 lemons; squeeze the juice from 4 lemons. Place all the ingredients in a jar and set aside to brine for 3 weeks before serving.

spicy pickled plums
Replace the pears with plums (halved and pitted).

variations

pickled shallots

see base recipe page 211

honeyed pickled shallots
Replace the vinegar with cider vinegar; replace the sugar with honey.

balsamic shallots
Replace the vinegar with dark balsamic vinegar.

clippy's soft pickled shallots
To make softer onions, pour the hot vinegar over the shallots.

spicy pickled shallots
Replace the spices with 4 dried habañero chilies and 1 teaspoon mustard seeds.

cider pickled shallots
Replace half the vinegar with cider vinegar and the remaining half with dry cider (non sparkling).

variations

classic piccalilli

see base recipe page 212

honeyed piccalilli
Replace 55g (2 oz) of the sugar with honey; add 1 teaspoon of dry roasted cumin seeds.

piccachili
Add 1 teaspoon dried chili flakes and 1 medium-sized chili pepper (sliced).

garlic piccalilli
Add 10 whole garlic cloves along with the vegetables.

indian piccalilli
Keep the cauliflower but swap the vegetables for cucumbers, red peppers, green tomatoes, and shallots. Add ½ teaspoon curry powder.

spiced piccalilli
Add extra spices — ¼ teaspoon celery seeds, 3 whole cloves, half a cinnamon stick, 1 bay leaf, and ¼ teaspoon of mixed spice.

variations

green bean pickle

see base recipe page 215

nasturtium & bay leaf pickle
Replace the green beans with nasturtium pods, the cider vinegar with white wine vinegar; add bay leaves instead of the tarragon.

pickled cucumbers
Replace the pods with cucumbers (skin on) cut so that they fit standing up in a jar. Replace the spices and herbs with ½ teaspoon mustard seed, ½ teaspoon dried chili flakes, and ¼ teaspoon ground turmeric.

dilly pickled cucumbers
Same recipe as above but add 1 teaspoon dill seed.

pickled asparagus
Make sure to use a jar tall enough for the asparagus. Omit the beans and spices/herbs. Replace with 2 sprigs fresh dill, ½ teaspoon dill seed, ½ teaspoon mustard seeds, 1 tablespoon nasturtium pods, and the zest from 1 lemon. Only brine the asparagus for 2 hours, and then follow the recipe.

variations

best-ever pickled eggs

see base recipe page 216

extra spicy pickled eggs
Add 2 whole red chilies when cooking the vinegar; add one to each jar.

balsamic pickled eggs
Replace the vinegar with balsamic vinegar.

chipotle pickled eggs
Omit the spices and replace them with chipotle (can use canned),
5 tablespoons of hot sauce, 4 cloves of crushed garlic, and 1 medium
white onion, sliced.

garlic pickled eggs
Omit the spices and replace them with 12 crushed garlic cloves and
1 medium red onion, sliced in rings; follow the recipe. Add the onion
rings after each egg.

pink pickled eggs
Omit the water and add red beetroot juice; add with the vinegar, etc.

variations

mostarda di frutta

see base recipe page 219

spicy mostarda di frutta
Replace yellow mustard seeds with black mustard seeds; replace the dried
fruits with equal amounts of pears, peaches, and quinces.

grape & rosemary mostarda
Replace the fruits with black/green grapes; add 1 tablespoon of freshly
chopped rosemary.

peach & cherry mostarda
Replace the fruits with equal amounts of peaches (skins removed) and
cherries (pitted); replace the honey with light brown sugar.

apple, pear & raspberry mostarda
Replace the fruit with equal amounts of apples/pears (peeled, cored,
chopped) and raspberries. Add the raspberries in the last 10 minutes of
cooking.

figgy mostarda di frutta
Replace all the dried fruits with whole baby dried figs; add 2 tablespoons of
Cognac just before potting. Replace the sugar with diabetic sugar.

chutneys

These mouth-watering delights will quickly become essential in any kitchen. A heady combination of fruit or vegetables with spices, herbs, vinegars, sugars, and dried fruits, are chopped small and cooked until you they reach a jam-like consistency. They're rich and flavoursome, and they'll add a special touch to any meal.

flaming mango chutney

see variations page 238

This is one of the first chutneys I ever made. Enjoy with a good curry or sizzling shrimp.

1 medium red onion (peeled)
450g (1 lb) cooking apples (weight once cored
  & peeled)
2 large garlic cloves, crushed
1 small red chili (diced)
1 tsp. ginger, freshly sliced

125ml (4½ fl. oz) cider vinegar
250g (9 oz) mango (once peeled, de-stoned)
  chopped
150g (5½ oz) granulated fructose
3½ tbsp. dry cider (optional)

Thinly slice the onion and chop the apples. Add all the ingredients to your pan (except the mango, sugar and dry cider); combine the ingredients and cook on a medium heat for about 10 minutes.

The mixture should start to get thick and juicy (stir frequently to prevent the chutney burning — especially in the first 5 minutes). Then add the chopped mango for approximately 5 minutes.

Once your 15–20 minute cook has finished, add the sugar and dry cider; stir until the sugar is dissolved. Crank up the heat and cook for another 15–20 minutes (watch your pan carefully; it should only simmer). The chutney should be quite thick and your mangoes should be soft but not squishy. Always taste your chutney before potting. If required, add additional spices for your personal taste. Spoon into sterilized jars. Use within 12 months.

Makes 500g (1 lb 2 oz)

spiced roasted plum chutney

see variations page 239

Roasting fruits for chutneys, intensifies both the flavour and colour of the chutney. I love trying out unorthodox ways of making preserves, and this one is made in the oven.

675g (1 lb 8 oz) plums (halved & pitted)
350g (12 oz) apples (peeled, cored & quartered)
200g (7 oz) onion (peeled & quartered)
200ml (7 fl. oz) apple cider vinegar
200ml (7 fl. oz) red wine vinegar
400g (14 oz) light brown muscovado sugar

1 cinnamon stick (broken in half)
2 star anise
½ tsp. roasted crushed coriander seeds
¼ tsp. yellow mustard seeds
10 cardamom pods (crushed)
½ tsp. crushed chili flakes

Preheat the oven to 160°C (325°F). Line a roasting pan, alternating between plum, apple, and onion. This will make sure that they will cook together, and the flavours will mingle together (make sure they are in lines and not on top of each other). Then pour the vinegars over the mixture and sprinkle the sugar on top. Add half the cinnamon at each end, along with the star anise. Sprinkle the other spices over the mixture. Place in the oven for approximately 1 hour; remove and check. It should be glossy and syrupy.

This recipe can take up to 3 hours to cook. You're looking for lovely soft fruit and onions in thick, glossy syrup. Remember that when this mixture cools, the syrup will be a lot thicker, so keep checking every so often to make sure it's not burning. If there is still too much liquid after 1½ hours, drain the juice and reduce on the stove, until thick and syrupy. Then add the syrup mixture back to the fruity mixture and cook until the syrup thickens. Spoon the chutney into clean, cool sterilized jars and sea. Mature for at least 2 weeks before serving.

Makes 600g (1 lb 5 oz)

cranapple chutney

see variations page 240

This is a must-have recipe for the holiday season. The marriage of popping cranberries and apples make this sublime chutney; serve with an array of holiday treats. You could also make this as a Christmas gift in a basket with cheese and crackers.

400g (14 oz) tart apples (weight when peeled,
    cored) chopped
400g (14 oz) cranberries
2 medium red onions, thinly sliced
1 large orange (zest & juice only)
1 large garlic clove, crushed
1 tsp. ginger (sliced thin)

1 cinnamon stick
250g (9 oz) light brown muscovado sugar
100ml (3½ fl. oz) red wine vinegar
3½ tbsp. mulled wine
pinch flaked salt
pinch freshly ground black pepper

Add the apples, cranberries, onions, orange juice, zest, garlic, ginger, and cinnamon stick to a large pan. Cook on a medium heat with a lid on for approximately 10–15 minutes; it's important to keep the lid on because the cranberries jump out of the pan when they are popping!

Once the cranberry skins are soft, add the sugar, vinegar, and mulled wine; stir until the sugar has dissolved. Cook the chutney until it resembles a thick jam. Add the flaked salt and freshly ground black pepper to taste and then spoon the chutney into cooled sterilized jars and seal. Store for a couple of weeks before opening.

Makes 1kg (2 lbs 4 oz)

pumpkin & ginger chutney

see variations page 241

Pumpkin for me is the champion of the vegetable world; its golden flesh makes a beautiful chutney. Serve alongside roast lamb and butterbean purée.

700g (1lb 9 oz) pumpkin (peeled and deseeded) chopped into cubes
2 medium red onions (peeled), sliced thinly
2 medium-sized pears (peeled, cored), chopped into cubes

400ml (13½ fl. oz) pear cider (dry)
100g (3½ oz) brown sugar
1 large piece ginger (peeled), sliced thinly
3 tbsp. preserved ginger
1 tbsp. ginger syrup

Place all the ingredients in a large pan and bring to a boil. Reduce the heat to a simmer and cook for about 1 hour, stirring occasionally. Once it resembles a thick jam, remove from the heat.

Ladle into cool, sterilized jars, seal, and store. Use within 6 months.

Makes 900g (2 lbs)

green tomato chutney

see variations page 242

This is the perfect recipe for tomatoes that just won't ripen before the first frost. Try adding to a winter stew or swirled through steamed rice.

600g (1 lb 5 oz) green tomatoes
1 large cooking apple (peeled & cored)
1 small green chili (seeds removed & sliced)
1 small shallot (peeled) sliced and diced

1 small piece ginger (peeled) sliced
1 large clove garlic (crushed & sliced)
200ml (7 fl. oz) white balsamic vinegar

Start by scoring the ends of the tomatoes. Place them in a bowl and pour over hot water over them. Let stand for 1–2 minutes, then peel.

Heat the sugar in a dry pan until the sugar melts and becomes caramelized. Add all the ingredients to the pan and bring to a boil. Reduce the heat and simmer for approximately 1 hour, or until you have a thick, jam-like consistency.

Remove from the heat and spoon into sterilized jars and seal.

Makes 650g (1 lb 7 oz)

roasted red pepper chutney

see variations page 243

The sweet smell of roasted peppers and the smoky paprika flavours are a winning combination. Team that with tomatoes and you're onto a surefire winner.

600g (1 lb 5 oz) large tomatoes (skinned)
5 large red peppers (roasted, skinned)
2 large shallots (peeled) diced
3 cloves garlic, crushed

1 pinch smoked paprika
200ml (7 fl. oz) red wine vinegar
2 medium-sized red chili peppers (sliced)
200g (7 oz) caster sugar

First score the ends of the tomatoes and place them in a bowl. Pour hot water over them until covered. Leave for 20 minutes and then peel. Let cool.

Cover the peppers in olive oil and roast in a preheated 170°C (350°F) oven for approximately 20–30 minutes, until the skin is charred. Remove and place in a paper bag until you can peel them; let cool.

Place the tomatoes, shallots, garlic, paprika, vinegar, and chili in a pan; cook for 10–15 minutes, until the tomatoes have lost their tarty bite and are starting to break down. Then add the sugar and chopped roasted peppers and cook for another 5–10 minutes.

Spoon the chutney into cool, sterilized jars and seal. Leave for a couple of weeks to let the flavours harmonize. Once opened, store in the refrigerator and eat within 6 weeks.

Makes 800g (1 lb 12 oz)

ruddy rhubarb & ginger chutney

see variations page 244

Serve with pan-fried mackerel or salmon with a side salad and sweet potato fries.

250g (9 oz) cooking apples (peeled, cored and
    chopped)
small handful sultanas
1 small red onion, peeled, sliced, and chopped
3½ tbsp. red wine vinegar

1 tsp. cinnamon
2 teaspoons ground ginger
3 teaspoons apple pie spice
150g (3½ oz) rhubarb, chopped
200g (7 oz) sugar

Add all the ingredients to your pan, except the sugar and rhubarb; combine and cook on medium heat for about 10 minutes. Add the rhubarb; cook gently until the mixture starts to get thick and juicy (stir frequently to prevent the chutney from burning — especially in the first 5 minutes).

Once your first cook has finished, add the sugar, and stir until the sugar is dissolved. Crank up the heat and cook for another 10–20 minutes (watch your pan carefully; it should only simmer).

Always taste your chutney before potting. If required, add additional spices for your personal taste. Spoon into sterilized jars and seal. Use within 12 months.

Makes 650g (1 lb 3 oz)

perfect apple chutney

see variations page 245

My love for apples started with my two apple trees in my garden, today I supply major UK supermarkets with my apple-based preserves. From my home kitchen to yours!

10 peppercorns
1 star anise
1 cinnamon stick
½ tsp. coriander seeds
½ tsp. cumin
¼ tsp. ground nutmeg
250ml (9 fl. oz) white wine vinegar

1kg (2lbs 4 oz) cooking apples (peeled, cored, and chopped weight)
225g (8 oz) banana shallots
150g (5½ oz) large sultanas
100g (3½ oz) light brown Muscavdo sugar
100g (3½ oz) sugar

Put the spices into a large pan and pour over the vinegar, cover, and gently simmer for approximately 30 minutes. Strain and discard the spices.

Into the same pan add the apples, shallots, sultanas, sugars, and spiced vinegar. Bring to the boil, then reduce the heat and simmer gently for approximately one hour until you have the consistency of a thick jam. If the apples look quite dry after 30 minutes add 1–2 tablespoons water and finish the remaining cook.

Remove from the heat and spoon into sterilized jars and seal. Leave to mature for a couple of weeks, once opened store in the refrigerator and use within 6 weeks.

Makes 1.2kg (2 lb 10 oz)

variations

flaming mango chutney

see base recipe page 227

super mango chutney
For a more indulgent chutney, omit the apples and top with mangoes.

flaming mango ginger chutney
Add 2 tablespoons of chopped stem ginger.

mango & lemon chutney
Add the zest and juice from 2 lemons when cooking the apples.

cranberry & mango flaming chutney
Replace half the apples with cranberries (remember to keep the lid on when cooking the cranberries).

variations

spiced roasted plum chutney

see base recipe page 228

all the plums chutney
Remove the onions and apples. Replace them with an equivalent amount of
plums. Add the zest of an orange just before you pot the chutney.

spiced plums & pears
Replace the apples with pears; omit the chilies.

ginger plum chutney
Omit the black mustard seeds and replace it with ground ginger; add an
additional teaspoon of freshly grated ginger.

hot, sweet, sticky plum chutney
Add 2 dried chilies when cooking the fruit; replace the sugar with dark
brown black treacle.

nutty spiced plum chutney
Add 120g (4 oz) unsalted pecans in the last hour of cooking.

variations

cranapple chutney

see base recipe page 230

blackberry apple chutney
Replace the cranberries with blackberries and keep the lid off when cooking.
Replace the vinegar with balsamic vinegar; proceed as main recipe.

cranorange chutney
Replace half the apples with the zest and juice from 2 large oranges. Add
this along with the remaining orange zest and juice.

cranberry quince chutney
Replace the apples with quince, and replace the mulled wine with honey.

cranapple chutney
Replace the vinegar with sherry vinegar; replace the sugar with demerara
sugar.

zesty lemon & cranberry chutney
Replace the orange with lemon; add 2 tablespoons of preserved lemons,
chopped (see pickling recipe page 220).

variations

pumpkin & ginger chutney

see base recipe page 231

pumpkin quince ginger chutney
Replace the pears with quince; change the pear cider to apple cider.

thai infused pumpkin chutney
Replace the pear cider with apple juice; omit the stem ginger and syrup and replace it with 1 red chili (diced), 2 tablespoons of lemongrass, ½ teaspoon of fresh mint, and ½ teaspoon of fresh coriander (add two at the end).

cider pumpkin chutney
Replace half the pear cider with cider vinegar and apple juice.

pumpkin & raisin chutney
Add 100g (3½ oz) raisins.

variations

green tomato chutney

see base recipe page 232

red & green tomato chutney
Replace half of the green tomatoes with red tomatoes; add these in the last 30 minutes of cooking.

roasted green tomato chutney
Roast the green tomatoes with a sprinkle of sugar and vinegar until soft, and then add to the apples.

indian green tomato chutney
Replace half the green tomatoes with sultanas and add ½ teaspoon ground cumin and ½ teaspoon ground coriander.

chargrilled pepper & tomato chutney
Chargrill 1 red pepper (skin and chop); add along with the remaining ingredients, and add 2 additional garlic cloves, roasted.

quince & green tomato chutney
Replace the apple with quince and replace the vinegar with white wine vinegar.

variations

roasted red pepper chutney

see base recipe page 235

apple pepper chutney
Replace the tomatoes with the same amount of cooking apples and proceed
as main recipe.

sweet pepper chutney
Replace the superfine sugar with light brown sugar for a more robust,
sweeter flavour. Roast the onions along with the peppers to increase the
sweetness.

pear pepper chutney
Replace half of the tomatoes with pears (cored, peeled, and chopped).

mango & red pepper chutney
Replace half the tomatoes with mango; replace the sugar with light brown
sugar; omit the paprika and replace it with cumin seeds.

variations

ruddy rhubarb & ginger chutney

see base recipe page 236

peachy peach & ginger chutney
Replace the rhubarb with the same weight of peaches (skinned, halved, and pitted).

rhubarb, almond & pear chutney
Replace the apples with pears; add 3 tablespoons of toasted flaked almonds at the end of cooking; omit the sultanas.

caramelized red onion & rhubarb chutney
Replace the apples with red onions and cook these for 20–30 minutes with a knob of butter and a tablespoon of sugar. Once cooked, add to the rhubarb.

curried rhubarb chutney
Omit the apple pie spice and add 1 teaspoon curry powder along with the zest from 1 lime.

perfect apple chutney

see base recipe page 237

perfect apple chutney
Replace the sultanas with chopped dates.

curried apple chutney
Omit the spices and replace them with 1 teaspoon curry powder and
1 teaspoon freshly chopped garlic and grated ginger.

appletastic chutney
Use whatever apples you can find; mince the onions and replace the cider
vinegar with white wine vinegar; use granulated sugar instead of the light
brown sugar.

apples & figs
Replace the dried fruit with baby figs (soaked overnight in apple juice; pulse
the following day to a figgy mush). Follow the recipe.

farmhouse apple chutney
Use a mix of apples, turnips, courgette, green peppers, turnips, and onions
(diced; they must all be the same size cubes).

condiments

Pass the ketchup! These tasty treats will get your

tastebuds tingling; try ketchups, mustards, honeyed

nuts, marinated vegetables, or cheeses in spiced oils.

Forget salt and pepper; everything you need to add

a big hit of flavour is right here in this chapter.

roasted tomatoes in olive oil

see variations page 269

Once you've tasted these little beauties, you'll never buy a can of tomatoes again. Use in pasta sauces or spread them onto pizza bases with mozzarella and fresh torn basil leaves.

1kg (2 lbs 4 oz) ripe tomatoes
pinch smoked flaked salt
pinch freshly ground black pepper
1 tbsp. light brown muscovado sugar
3 tbsp. red wine vinegar

2 cloves organic garlic
1 medium green chili, fresh
12–15 whole black peppercorns
5 fresh bay leaves (whole not broken)
enough canola oil to top off the jar

Halve the tomatoes and place them on a wire rack; sprinkle with the salt, pepper, and sugar. Set aside for 15 minutes. Place the rack over a baking tray to collect all the juices and put them in a 175°C (350°F) oven for about 1–2 hours — depending on how juicy they are. Check the tomatoes to make sure they haven't dried out too much — they will reduce but should still remain plump. Once you get to this stage, let them cool for about 20–30 minutes and pour the vinegar over them. Meanwhile, thinly slice the garlic cloves and slice the chili.

Start by layering your tomatoes in the jar; add a few slivers of garlic, chili, some black peppercorns, and a bay leaf. Repeat this process until the jar is full. Carefully pour in the juices and the canola oil until you reach the rim of the sterilized jar. Screw the lid on tightly. Use within 5 days (keep somewhere cool and dark).

Makes 450g (1 lb)

honeyed mixed nuts

see variations page 270

Fill a bowl with fresh cut strawberries & blueberries, a big dollop of natural yogurt, and a couple of spoonfuls of these honeyed nuts for a super-charged healthy breakfast.

125g (4½ oz) pecans
125g (4½ oz) walnuts
125g (4½ oz) hazelnuts

125g (4½ oz) almonds
125g (4½ oz) macadamia nuts
600g 1 lb 5 oz of your favourite runny honey

First, dry-roast the nuts: preheat the oven to 175°C (350°F), place the nuts in single layers of a couple of baking pans and gently roast for 4–5 minutes. Make sure you give the pan a good jiggle so that the nuts don't burn. Let them cool; this will make sure that the nuts are still crunchy when you eat them.

Place a layer of nuts, then 2 tablespoons of honey, in a sterilized jar. Add another layer of nuts, then 2 more tablespoons of honey. Repeat until the jar is jam-packed with nuts. Make sure all nuts are covered with the honey.

Keep sealed and leave in a cool dark place for up to a week.

Makes 1 large jar

marinated goat's cheese

see variations page 271

For a perfect lunch, serve the marinated cheese with a simple green salad and use the herb, garlic, and chili oil as a dressing. Don't use extra-virgin olive oil, it solidifies when cold and doesn't look very pretty in the jar; good-quality virgin oil is best here.

3 fresh goat's cheeses, each weighing 1¾ oz
    with full rind left on
2 pinches saffron
2 whole garlic cloves

1 litre (1¾ pints) good-quality olive oil
2 medium chilies (sliced)
2 fresh bay leaves
10 whole black peppercorns

Unwrap the goat's cheeses and place them in a sterilized Kilner jar. Place the remaining ingredients in a separate jar or bottle with a tight-fitting lid. Seal. Shake to mix well, then gently pour the saffron, garlic, and chili oil over the goat's cheeses.

Store in the refrigerator for at least 1 week before serving. Use within 3 weeks of opening.

Makes 1 x 500g (1 lb 2 oz) Kilner jar

marinated mediterranean delicacies

see variations page 272

This is another Christmas-inspired recipe. I often make my own presents and this preserve is a welcome addition to a hamper full of food goodies. Don't be tempted to use extra-virgin olive oil; it solidifies when cold and doesn't look very pretty in the jar.

1 pack feta cheese (¾ lb), cubed
3 slices halloumi cheese (whole slices), grilled
handful good-quality olives with pits
1 red pepper, roasted, skinned, and sliced

3 whole garlic cloves
3 fresh bay leaves
2 medium red chilies, sliced
500ml (17 fl. oz) good-quality olive oil

Place some cubes of feta, a slice of halloumi, a few olives, and a few slices of roasted peppers, garlic clove, bay leaf and some chilies in a sterilized Kilner jar. Pour some of the olive oil over the cheese mixture and repeat this process until the cheeses are covered in oil.

Store in the refrigerator for at least 1 week. It will keep for about 1-2 weeks in the refrigerator.

Makes 1 x 500g (1 lb 2 oz) Kilner jar

spiced cranberry sauce

see variations page 273

What would turkey be without cranberry sauce? This also goes brilliantly with rich cheeses and cured meats.

600g (1 lb 5 oz) fresh/frozen cranberries
2 large juicy oranges, plus zest
300g (10½ oz) raw cane sugar

2 cinnamon sticks
5 cloves

Wash the cranberries and place them in a saucepan. Wash the orange and remove the zest. Keep a long piece of peel and stud it with the cloves; very finely chop the rest of the zest. Squeeze the orange and add the juice, zest, and pulp to the cranberries. Add the sugar and spices; stir well.

Bring to a gentle simmer with the lid on, because the cranberries can jump out of the pan. Stir to dissolve the sugar. Taste the sauce at this stage. If you find the sauce is too tart for your taste, add a little more sugar.

Cover and simmer for 15 minutes, until the cranberries are soft and splitting. Some of them will cook more quickly than others. Don't forget to stir the sauce every few minutes. When the sauce is ready, spoon into sterilized jars.

Makes 450g (1 lb)

spiced plum ketchup

see variations page 274

One of my all-time favourites, this is a silky piquant sauce that's full of flavour and depth. The commercial varieties of ketchup are not a patch on the homemade variety.

900g (2 lbs) plums (halved & pitted)
300g (10½ oz) onions (peeled & quartered)
300ml (10½ fl. oz) cider vinegar
300ml (10½ fl. oz) red wine vinegar
500g (1 lb 2 oz) light brown muscovado sugar

1 tsp. ground cinnamon
½ tsp. roasted coriander seeds, crushed
¼ tsp. yellow mustard seeds
2 garlic cloves (peeled), chopped
2 tbsp. maple syrup

Preheat your oven to 175°C (325°F). Lay the plums and onions in lines in a roasting pan alternating between plum and onion. This will make sure that they will cook together and that the flavours mingle. Pour half of each vinegar over the mixture and sprinkle the sugar, ground cinnamon, coriander seeds, mustard seeds, and chopped garlic over the mixture. Place in the oven for approximately 1 hour. Remove and check; it should be glossy and syrupy.

Cook for up to 3 hours, until the fruit and onions are soft, in thick glossy syrup. Remove the mixture once the plums and onions are really soft and the juices have turned into syrup. Then rub the mixture through a nylon sieve (you will need a nylon sieve to push through the plums; do not use stainless steel because this changes the colour and taste of the finished ketchup). Return the purée to a pan and add the remaining vinegars. Bring the mixture to a boil and simmer until you have the consistency of ketchup. Spoon the ketchup into clean, cool sterilized jars and seal. Mature for at least 2 weeks before serving.

Makes 600g (1 lb 5 oz)

blackberry ketchup

see variations page 275

This ketchup is very rich, tasty and downright lip-smacking. Try using a couple of tablespoons to liven up sauces or try adding to a ragu for a homemade lasagna.

10 peppercorns	250ml (9 fl. oz) white wine vinegar
1 star anise	1kg (2 lbs 4 oz) blackberries
1 cinnamon stick	125ml (4½ fl. oz) apple juice
½ tsp. coriander seeds	125g (4½ oz) demerara or brown sugar
¼ tsp. cumin seeds	pinch smoked salt
¼ nutmeg	pinch fresh ground black pepper

First make the spiced vinegar: Put the spices into a pan and pour the vinegar over them; cover and gently heat. Do not boil. Simmer for approximately 30 minutes. Strain and discard the spices.

Cook the blackberries with the apple juice until they have the consistency of a purée. Rub the blackberry mixture through a nylon sieve (do not use stainless steel because it changes the colour and taste of the finished ketchup). Transfer the purée to a clean pan and add the sugar and spiced vinegar; bring to a boil. Simmer until you a get a thick consistency; add the seasoning. Spoon the ketchup into sterilized bottles with screw caps/lids. Use within 4 months.

Makes 750g (1 lb 10 oz)

proper tomato ketchup

see variations page 276

The king of all ketchups is the Tomato; this is a handy recipe for using up a glut of tomatoes. This tomato ketchup is perfect dunked into homemade fries with a sprinkle of salt & vinegar.

1kg (2 lbs 4 oz) ripe tomatoes
pinch smoked flaked salt
1/4 tsp. freshly ground black pepper
1/4 tsp. mustard powder
1/2 tsp. celery salt

1/4 tsp. ground cloves
1 clove organic garlic, finely chopped
2 whole bay leaves
125g (41/2 oz) light brown muscovado sugar
6 tbsp. red wine vinegar

Halve the tomatoes and place them on a wire rack; sprinkle with the salt, pepper, spices, and garlic. Set aside for 15 minutes. Place the rack over a baking tray to collect all the juices and place in a 175°C (350°F) oven for 1–2 hours — depending on how juicy they are. Check the tomatoes to make sure they haven't dried out too much — they will reduce but should still remain plump. Once you get to this stage, let them cool for about 20–30 minutes.

Rub the tomatoes through a nylon sieve (do not use stainless steel because this changes the colour and taste of the finished ketchup). Transfer the purée to a clean pan and add the sugar and vinegar; bring to a boil. Simmer until you a get a thick consistency; add the seasoning. If you feel it needs more sugar or vinegar, taste and adjust accordingly. Pour the ketchup into sterilized bottles with screw caps/lids. Use within 1 month.

Makes 450g (1 lb)

choc o'cherry sauce

see variations page 277

Delicious with pancakes, served with vanilla ice cream, or sandwiched between sponge cakes.

400g (1 lb 12 oz) cherries (whole)
1½ tbsp. water
420g (15 oz) white cane sugar

235g (8 ½ oz) dark chocolate (use at least 70 percent cocoa solids), coarsely chopped
4 tbsp. Kirsch

Put the cherries and the water into the pan, and simmer gently until the fruit softens. Do not overcook; they are very delicate. You should be able to remove the stones at this point. I leave the stones in because they impart an almond flavour to the sauce, and it's easier than de-stoning the cherries.

Add the sugar and stir until dissolved. Cook rapidly for 5 minutes, and then add the chocolate. Once it has melted, remove from the heat add the Kirsch.

Cool the sauce for 5–10 minutes; stir and pour into sterilized jars. Once potted, store in the refrigerator and consume within 3 months.

Makes 1kg (2 lbs 4 oz)

christmas figgy boozy mincemeat

see variations page 278

So what is mincemeat? Homemade mincemeat is a traditional sweet preserve consisting of a mixture of dried fruits, tart apples, brown sugar, suet, spices heavily doused in rum or brandy. The mincemeat is brought together and spooned into all-butter pastry cases, topped with a pastry lid and baked until crisp.

200g (7 oz) sultanas
200g (7 oz) raisins
75g (3 oz) figs, chopped
75g (3 oz) candied peel
75g (3 oz) dried apricots, chopped
75g (3 oz) glacé cherries, chopped
1/4 tsp. cinnamon
1 orange, zested and juiced

3 1/2 tbsp. preserved ginger, chopped
2 tbsp. ginger syrup
1 large cooking apple (peeled & cored) grated
200g (7 oz) vegetarian suet
200g (7 oz) light brown muscovado sugar
1/2 tsp. apple pie spice
100ml (3 1/2 fl. oz) brandy

Add all the ingredients (expect the brandy) into a large ovenproof (non-metallic) bowl, and mix until well combined. Cover loosely with foil and store in a dark, cool place overnight.

Preheat the oven to 150°C (300°F) and place the bowl in the oven for 2–3 hours. You'll notice a layer of fat from the suet. This is what you're looking for; it will coat all the ingredients, and the mincemeat will be less likely to ferment. Remove from the oven and let cool. Stir every so often to make sure all the mixture is coated in the melted suet.

When the mincemeat is cold, stir vigorously and add the brandy. Pack the mincemeat into sterilized jars; seal and store. Use within 1 year of making.

Makes 1kg (2 lbs 4 oz)

three apple & cider sauce

see variations page 279

This is the best apple sauce ever, I promise! I often make this a couple of days ahead. It's perfect with grilled pork chops, with crumbly white cheeses, or as a topping for French toast or vanilla ice cream.

knob of butter
500g (1 lb 2 oz) apples (peeled & cored)
   chopped

100ml (3½ fl. oz) dry cider
1 tbsp. cider vinegar
150g (5½ oz) sugar

Add the butter to the pan. Once melted, add the apples and cider to the pan and simmer gently for 10 minutes.

Add the vinegar and sugar; combine. Once the sugar has dissolved, heat for 5 minutes. Transfer to a sterilized jar and seal. Place in the refrigerator and use within 1 week.

Makes 500g (1 lb 2 oz)

homemade sticky barbecue sauce

see variations page 280

This recipe uses the tomato ketchup recipe on page 261, and some of my favourite spices with a little tickle of rum. This sticky sauce is so tasty, your chicken wings and baby back ribs will be begging for more.

3 tbsp. peanut oil
1 small white onion (finely diced
1 small red bell pepper (finely diced)
2 cloves garlic (crushed & finely diced)
3 tbsp. dark rum
1½ tbsp. chili powder
½ tbsp. ground cloves
¼ tsp. ground spice

½ tbsp. ground black pepper
2 tbsp. mustard powder
235g (8½ oz) Proper Tomato Ketchup (page 261)
100g (3½ oz) dark brown muscovado sugar
235ml (8½ fl. oz) apple juice
3 tbsp. cider vinegar
3 tbsp. black treacle

Heat the peanut oil and add the onion, peppers, garlic, and a pinch of salt. Cook on medium heat until the onions are soft but not brown. Add the rum and cook for another 2 minutes. Add the spices and let them mingle for a few minutes. Add the remaining ingredients and cook for another 20–30 minutes, until it becomes thick, dark, and intensely juicy.

Remove from the heat, pour into a food processor, and blend the sauce to a purée. Season to taste and pour into warm, sterilized bottles with screw-top lids or stoppers. Store in the refrigerator and use within 4 weeks.

Makes 700g (1 lb 8 oz)

wholegrain honey mustard

see variations page 281

This simple recipe is easy to follow, and you can play with the ingredients to come up with your own style of mustard. There's no cooking involved, just standing time.

350g (12½ oz) yellow mustard seeds
250g (9 oz) brown mustard seeds
250ml (9 fl. oz) cider vinegar
1 stick cinnamon (split in two)

pinch crushed chili flakes
½ tsp. flaked salt
7 tbsp. runny honey

Place the the yellow and brown mustard seeds in a medium-sized bowl with the cider vinegar, cinnamon stick, flaked salt, and chili flakes. Cover and leave in a cool, dark place for 24–48 hours. The seeds will swell; if it becomes too dry, add some extra liquid.

Remove and discard the cinnamon stick; gently combine the honey with the mustard seeds until gooey and sticky. Transfer a third of the mixture to a food processor and pulse until you have a thick paste. Add the paste to the mustard seeds and combine. Spoon into cool sterilized jars and seal. Use within 6 months.

Makes 700g (1 lb 8 oz)

variations

roasted tomatoes in olive oil

see base recipe page 247

roast pepper in olive oil
Replace the tomatoes with a selection of green, red, and yellow peppers. Cut the peppers in half and continue with the recipe.

roasted chilies in olive oil
Replace the tomatoes with an equal quantity of large chilies. Remove the seeds for a mild preserve, or keep them for a spicy preserve.

roasted courgettes in olive oil
Replace the tomatoes with courgettes. Slice the courgettes lengthways into long ribbons (use a vegetable peeler) and proceed as the main recipe.

roasted tomatoes in basil oil
Replace the canola oil with a very light olive oil, and substitute the chili and the bay leaves with a small handful whole, unblemished, fresh basil leaves.

variations

honeyed nuts

see base recipe page 249

cinnamon honeyed nuts
When dry roasting the nuts, add a pinch of your favourite spice, such as cinnamon, vanilla pod seeds, mixed spice, etc.

honey-roasted almonds
Preheat oven to 180°C (350°F) and line a baking sheet with foil. Rub or spray foil with a little oil. In a medium saucepan heat 2 tablespoons clear honey, 1 tablespoon maple syrup, and 1½ tablespoons unsalted butter, until the butter is just melted. Remove from the heat and stir in 1 teapsoon salt and 1 teaspoon cinnamon. Add 450g (1 pound) whole, raw almonds and stir to coat all of the nuts. Spread on the prepared cookie sheet in a single layer and bake for 6 minutes. Remove from oven, turn nuts over, and place back in the oven for 6 more minutes. Remove from the oven, pour into a clean bowl, and toss with 2 tablespoons of sugar. Let cool, stirring occasionally. When completely cool pour into a glass jar with an airtight lid. Store in a cool, dark place for up to 2 weeks.

variations

marinated goat's cheese

see base recipe page 250

dried-chili infused goat's cheeses
Replace the fresh chilies with dried chilies for an intense, spicy oil.

herb-infused goat's cheeses
Replace the chilies with 2 sprigs fresh rosemary, chopped, and 1 tablespoon
fresh oregano leaves (chopped if large; whole if small).

herb-infused goat's cheeses and sun-blushed tomatoes in oil
Add 120g (4 oz) sun-blushed tomatoes with the goat's cheeses.

variations

marinated mediterranean delicacies

see base recipe page 253

marinated mediterranean delights with preserved lemons
Add 3 preserved lemons to the mix.

marinated olives
Omit the feta and halloumi cheeses, and increase the total weight of olives to 450g (1 lb).

minted marinated mediterranean delicacies
Omit the peppers and chilies, and add 2 tablespoons chopped fresh mint.

variations

spiced cranberry sauce

see base recipe page 254

spiced port & cranberry sauce
Add a glug of port or sherry at the end of cooking; stir in and pot.

clementine & cranberry sauce
Replace the oranges with the juice and zest of six small clementines.

spiced cranberry & chocolate muffins
Preheat the oven to 200°C (400°F). In a large bowl, mix 200g (7 oz) plain flour, ½ teaspoon salt, 2 teaspoons baking powder, ¼ teaspoon cinnamon, 100g (2½ oz) caster sugar, and 1 tablespoon orange zest. In a separate bowl, mix 125ml (4½ fl. oz) canola oil, 1 medium egg, 100ml (3½ fl. oz) milk, and 1 teaspoon vanilla extract. Mix the liquid into the dry ingredients, and stir through 120g (4 oz) dark chocolate chips. Spoon 1½ tablespoons of the batter into each of 12 muffin cases set into a muffin pan. Add a couple of tablespoons of the cranberry sauce to each muffin case, then divide the remaining batter between the muffin cases. Bake for 15–20 minutes or until golden.

variations

spiced plum ketchup

see base recipe page 257

cranapple ketchup
Replace the plums with half cranberries and half cooking apples. Remember, the cranberries will pop in the oven so place a sheet of baking paper over the top; remove once the juices start flowing.

spiced cherry ketchup
Replace the plums with an equal quantity of pitted dark cherries.

roasted duck & plum ketchup wraps
Serve the plum ketchup in a tortilla wrap with roasted, sliced duck breasts and lettuce, thinly sliced cucumber, and thinly sliced spring onions.

variations

blackberry ketchup

see base recipe page 258

blackberry lemon zing ketchup
Add the zest of 1 lemon when cooking the blackberries; this will give it a lemony zip.

gooseberry ketchup
Replace the blackberries with the same quantity of (preferably slightly underripe) gooseberries, topped and tailed.

very berry ketchup
Replace 225g (8 oz) of the blackberries with the same weight of blueberries.

variations

proper tomato ketchup

see base recipe page 261

spicy tomato ketchup
Add several dried chilies when roasting the tomatoes; retain and add back to the purée and discard before potting.

bloody mary ketchup
Add a glug of vodka in the final cook.

yellow tomato ketchup
Simply replace the fresh tomatoes with an equal quantity of yellow cherry tomatoes or yellow heirloom tomatoes.

variations

choc o'cherry sauce

see base recipe page 262

chocolate berry berry sauce
Replace the cherries with 280g (10 oz) strawberries and 280g (10 oz)
blueberries.

white chocolate & raspberry sauce
Replace the cherries with 450g (1 lb) fresh raspberries, replace the dark
chocolate with white chocolate, reduce the sugar to 250g (9 oz), and replace
the Kirsch with framboise.

choc o'cherry sauce (no alcohol)
Replace the Kirsch with apple juice.

variations

christmas figgy boozy mincemeat

see base recipe page 263

nutty rum mincemeat

Replace half the raisins with your favourite chopped dry roasted nuts; I love walnuts or pecans. Replace the brandy with rum.

alcohol-free christmas figgy mincemeat

Replace all of the brandy with apple juice.

easy mince pies

Preheat the oven to 180°C (375°F). Dust a worktop with flour, and roll out 1 package all-butter shortcrust pastry to 5-mm (¼-in.) thickness. With cookie cutters, cut twelve 7.5-cm (3-in.) circles and twelve 4-cm (1½-in.) circles. Place one large pastry circle in each hole of a shallow muffin pan. Place 1½ teaspoons Christmas Figgy Boozy Mincemeat into each pastry base, and then press a small pastry circle on the top of each pie. Seal all of the pies, and brush with a little beaten egg. Bake for 12–15 minutes until the pastry is cooked and the tops are golden.

variations

three apple & cider sauce

see base recipe page 264

spiced apple & cider sauce
Add ¼ teaspoon cinnamon, ¼ teaspoon nutmeg, and ½ teaspoon apple pie spice to the apples.

apple & apple brandy sauce
Reduce the quantity of apple cider to 55ml (2 fl. oz), and add 55ml (2 fl. oz) apple brandy (e.g. Calvados).

pear & apple sauce
Substitute half the apples for the same weight of firm, slightly underripe pears.

variations

homemade sticky barbecue sauce

see base recipe page 267

hot to trot barbecue sauce
Add 2 tablespoons of smoky hot sauce at the end of cooking.

homemade fruity barbecue sauce
Replace the tomato ketchup with an equal quantity of the Blackberry Ketchup on page 258.

extra-smoky sticky barbecue sauce
Add 1 teaspoon liquid smoke at the end of cooking.

variations

wholegrain honey mustard

see base recipe page 268

guinness wholegrain mustard
Replace the cider vinegar and soak with the same amount of Guinness.

blood orange wholegrain honey mustard
Replace the cider vinegar with the same quantity of blood orange juice.

spicy wholegrain honey mustard
Add 1 whole chipotle chili to the food processor with the third of the honey mustard. Proceed as main recipe.

wholegrain honey mustard vinaigrette
Whisk 55ml (2 fl. oz) white wine vinegar with 1 tablepoon wholegrain honey mustard. Whisk in 165ml (6 fl. oz) light oil (canola is good), and season to taste with salt and black pepper. Use to dress green salads.

index